Esoteric Publishing without the Corporate Control

Ordem dos Cavaleiros Maçons Elus Cohens do Universo
LOJA SOD HA OLAM - RIO DE JANEIRO - BRASIL

A Manual on Kabbalah in the Brazilian Tradition of the Elus Coen.

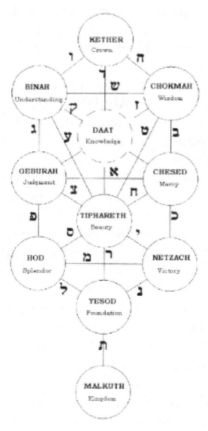

Introduction

After acquiring an archive of a well known Martinist order it was discovered that the Estatic Kabbalah was actually practiced in the Brazilian branch of the Elus Coen.

Some introductory remarks should probably be made to contextualize this translation. It has extensive footnotes to primarily spanish kabbalah so those have been omitted since many cannot acquire such texts. I do have an archive of English Abulafia texts, but those are still copyrighted so we cannot offer them with this publication.

A private reprint is available for members of the Ordre des Coëns Ressuscités. In our order we are able to now put a strong flag down for the Kabbalistic Tradition of Spain.

It seems from the first read of this document that it is in the line of Ecstatic Kabbalah of Abulafia and others. It mentions specific practices that are aimed at making Elus Coen materials more understandable through practice. Along with this document there is profound implications embedded. This is to my knowledge the first time a traditional Golem was connected to the Augoides, by saying that the Golem was essentially created by the Breath and Vibrational evocation of the Coen, we are able to move into the area of instruction for the Psalms which will accompany future work in the field of the Elus Coen.

This is the main benefit of this book. It contextualizes many subtle kabbalistic terms without drawing attention to itself. Also, for those interested it grounds the concept of "nothingness" which is probably tohu et vohu in the original bible into a seperate form of Identity. This is quite remarkable since it states there are two identities. This relates to modern psychological theory so well, that no other explantory information should be needed for the discerning reader.

This is not the first time that the Hebrew Letters have been mentioned this way either, but it's a definite proven fact that the Brazilian Coen was aware of this particular view of the 22 Hebrew Letters and most importantly they know why.

In this volume you will see that the letters are exacting because they have a special vibratory element to them. A precise science, the correspondances cannot be altered to get maximum effect from the material.

What shocks me is this has been known and at least in it's seed form made available to initiates since the time of Abulafia.

Along with the Dietary, Prayer work and now the Vibratory practices of what was known as "Niggunim" in Spain, we are able to put together a whole regimen of Coen practice that is focused upon the development and expansion of these metaphysical hypostases.

Of course this is just an introduction to the thought in this book, but it's a very powerful addition to the Illuminism of Spanish Coen, and probably published in English for the first time.

May it's pages light up that which was never darkened

Timothy Wright
Winter, 2025

INDEX

PREFACE

In this book, we propose a lesser-known yet fundamental aspect of Jewish mysticism: the practice of meditation.

This appendage of Judaism has been so hidden and repressed that, to specialists, it appears as a delusion or heresy. However, there exists a meditative mysticism, whose most famous representative was undoubtedly Rabbi Abraham Abulafia (1240–1292), who left us numerous treatises on the subject.

To begin studying Abulafia's work, one should consult the works and research of Moshe Idel, the successor to Gershom Scholem at the Kabbalah chair of the Hebrew University of Jerusalem. In particular, one should read his work L'Expérience mystique d'Abraham Abulafia, published by Cerf in 1989. In fact, Hebrew meditation can be traced back to the 1st century, the dawn of the Talmudic period.

It has discreetly traversed the centuries, passed down from master to disciple in almost absolute secrecy.

The Hasidim ("pious men") of medieval Germany, under the guidance of Rabbi Yehudah the Pious, developed and practiced many meditation exercises, most of them centered around the combinatory recitation of the Names of God.

It is worth noting in passing that it was within the German Hasidic circle that the legend of the Golem, a creature of clay animated by the breath of prayer, study, and meditation, developed. The idea of a magical power and the effectiveness of God's mysterious names giving life to a creature should be understood as a particularly sublime experience, tested through the mysticism contained in the mysteries of alphabetic combinations described in the Sefer Yetzirah (Book of Formation).

At that time, the original conception of the Golem seemed to suggest that it was only animated during its creator's ecstasy. It was only later that the legend attributed the Golem with an existence outside of the ecstatic consciousness.

Our interpretation of the Golem is both different and similar to these conceptions. The Golem is not another creature but the very man who becomes animated by a vital energy breathed into him through the combination of language and the letters of the Divine Name.

Originally, the Golem did not refer to this magical creature endowed with supernatural powers. The term "Golem" actually designates a handful of clay or other shapeless matter — matter animated, into which the breath of life, soul, and spirit must be introduced. The Golem is, therefore, a body, a lifeless statue awaiting life.

Man is placed within this "dialectic of the Golem," an alternation between an existence lacking fundamental vitality and a life fully energized by the dynamic movement of a project born from the constantly moving language.

We will do our best to present Hebrew meditation, revisiting the great texts of meditative mysticism and offering an anthology that, starting with the vision of the prophet Ezekiel (7th century BCE), will conclude with Rabbi Aaron Roth's Treatise on the Agitation of the Soul (Hungary, 1894–1944), passing through the pages of the Talmud, Maimonides (Spain, 1135–1204), Rabbi Eleazar of Worms (Germany, 1165–1230), the Zohar (13th century), Rabbi Isaac Luria and Rabbi Hayyim Vital (1542–1620), Moshe Hayyim Luzzatto (1707–1746), Rabbi Shalom Sharabi (1720–1777), Baal Shem Tov (1700–1750), the letters on ecstasy by Rabbi Dov Baer of Lubavitch (1773–1827), and Rabbi Isaac Eizik of Komarno (1806–1879).

We prefer to approach Hebrew meditation from a branch of Judaism that has practiced and developed it extensively. This branch sprang from Polish Hasidism, founded by the legendary figure of Baal Shem Tov, the Master of the Good

Name.

As Scholem rightly said, "Hasidism is the final phase in the evolution of Jewish mysticism," and although we may not fully identify with this movement, we are heirs to its spirit and methods.

The Hasidic movement itself comprises several currents. For many years, I have followed and taught the Hasidic philosophy of Rabbi Nachman of Breslov (1772–1810), the last grandson of Baal Shem Tov, who, more than anyone else, developed meditation under the generic name Hitbodédut.

After extensive experimentation with meditative practice, we concluded that meditation exercises not accompanied by constant study of the texts of the Tradition—Bible, Talmud, Zohar, etc.—quickly lead to the desiccation of the spirit and the very meditation itself. Study is the motor of meditation, even if the latter may not be a study in itself.

Therefore, this book is divided into three distinct parts, each of which requires the others to resonate all the harmonics of each subject.

The first part, entitled "Journeys of a Spark," briefly exposes the historical foundations of Hasidism, its origins in the Kabbalah of Rabbi Isaac Luria, and the adventures of the false messianism of Shabbetai Tzvi. It then presents the fundamental themes of Luria's Kabbalah, which left Hasidism with the philosophical and theological core of its worldview. This core opens up for us through a more general reflection on the current meaning of Hasidism.

One must avoid making the mistake of equating Hasidism with the orthodoxy as it appears today, as Hasidism is, in fact, the opposite of it, even though the followers of the Hasidic movement are also practitioners of Jewish rituals.

It is possible to be a Hasid without entering the sociological category of the Hasidic movement and be inspired by Hasidic thought, as is the case, for example, with Martin Buber, Abraham Yehoshua Herschel, Elie Wiesel, Haïm Potok, and, more indirectly, Kafka and even Woody Allen.

Contemporary Jewish culture cannot ignore that the legacy of Hasidism has renewed the breath of thought and practice (including art and music) within Judaism.

The second part of the book, "The Dancing Wisdom of Hasidism," is dedicated to the art of reading. Hasidism, like Kabbalah and the Talmud, is, in essence, a very particular art of reading and interpreting texts. It is an existential study in which man invents himself as he invents new meanings of being. A new man within a tradition of the new.

What we propose in this second part applies to all great Hebrew texts. In them, there is an "art of reading" that is, in essence, a decompositional practice, whose goal is to put language in motion, allowing man to inscribe himself in a ceaseless dynamic of meaning.

The consequences of this "art of reading" are multiple: philosophical, political, and therapeutic. Reading, as interpretation and raising the conflicts of interpretations, takes us out of the logic of truth and introduces us into a logic of meaning, or the "wisdom of uncertainty," which, as Kundera said about the novel, marks modernity. Politically, this opposes ideologies that are entirely grounded, even those that are well-intentioned, in the illusion of possessing the truth.

The "art of reading" we propose is summarized in the formula "read in pieces," which means breaking what is definitive to open up to the infinitive. The search for a beyond of the "identity enclosed in itself" that is incapable of advancing on the paths of the future.

The "art of reading" is a method that opens and liberates. The great specificity of Hebrew texts is the result of incessant work on language, a metalanguage of a metalanguage; the objective is not to understand better but to be caught in the rhythm of life, energy constantly in motion, driven by the rhythm of language.

In the course of our searches on this "art of reading" and in the practice of these interpretative methods, we have analyzed the impact that these interpretations and the very interpretative processes produced on listeners and co-interpreters. We have found, without ambiguity, an effect of opening, unclogging, relief, and at the same time, dynamism. In a word, the "read in pieces" method has allowed us to discover the therapeutic effects of reading and interpretation.

Thus, it is possible to literally speak of "bibliotherapy," meaning the healing by the book.

We believe that one of the essential functions of the biblical, Talmudic, and Midrashic text is to produce a set of mythical narratives, that is, those with the strength to structure dialectically and dynamically an identity, which will be called precisely "narrative identity."

Without delving into the complex details of this therapeutic method, which will be the subject of a forthcoming work, we wish to show in the third part of this book the main outlines of the relationship between meditation (study, interpretation) and holiness.

This third part is entitled "Body and Writing," because it highlights, based on texts from Hebrew mysticism, a relationship between the body and the letters of the Hebrew alphabet and between the body and language in general. Man is not man because of a "human nature," but thanks to an advance, a negation of that nature that leads to nothing but a supernature that builds the human and the person as a being responsible for their freedom.

This advance and access to this supernature is essentially

possible through language. But in this case, it is not the mouth that speaks. The man, in his complete constitution, "body-soul-spirit," constantly emits linguistic signs that mediate his relationship with the world and with life.

The motivating reading of meditation, derived from the Hebrew tradition, is: "a language in motion for a being in motion."

Through the act of meditating, vocalizing, and breathing in rhythm with the movements of language, which forms and unforms incessantly, Hebrew meditation acquires its meaning.

To do this, we will deepen the elementary structure of language and Hebrew writing, grounded in the point, line, and plane.

The exercises we present at the end of the book cannot be well executed and practiced unless based on a good knowledge of the theoretical aspects that we will first show. They are simple and within reach of everyone. They will not intervene in prior knowledge outside of the perfect knowledge of the letters of the Hebrew alphabet.

May this brief introduction, now, truly mark a new beginning for the soul.

FIRST PART
TRAVELS OF A SPARK

"The wise seek wisdom, the fool finds it."
G. C. Lichtenberg

CHAPTER I

Hasidism Today

"When Baal Shem Tov, Master of the Good Name and founder of Hasidism, had a difficult task before him or sensed that a disaster was being plotted against the Jewish people, he would withdraw to a certain place in the forest; there, he would light a fire, meditate in prayer, and whatever he had decided to accomplish became possible: the miracle occurred, the disaster was averted.

A generation later, when his disciple, the Maggid of Mezritch, had to intervene with Heaven for the same reasons as his predecessor, he would go to the same place in the forest and say:
"Master of the Universe, hear me. I no longer know how to light the fire, but I am still able to say the prayer."
And the miracle happened again.

In the next generation, Rabbi Moshe Lev of Sassov, to save his people, would also go to the forest and say:
"I no longer know how to light the fire, I no longer know the prayer, but I know the place, that should be enough."
And it was enough.
Then it was Rabbi Israel of Rizhin's turn to avert the threat. He sat in his golden armchair, at the heart of his castle. He put his head in his hands and turned to God:
"Master of the World, I am incapable of lighting the fire, I no longer know the prayer, nor can I even find the place in the forest. All I know how to do is to tell this story, that should be

13

enough."
And again, the miracle happened…

And now, we too are faced with the infinite responsibility to continue passing on the spark, the fire, and the story of the narrative.

The village replaced the forest, a library became our castle, but Hasidism remains alive.

We are all descendants of the great-grandchildren of Baal Shem Tov, this Master of the Good Name, descendants of the grandsons of Rabbi Israel, descendants of the sons of Eliezer, who taught us that man did not exist, but that he must invent himself. This is Hasidism.

Hasidism is not a doctrine, but a force, a breath that, incessantly, reminds man that his perfection lies in his perfectibility.
Certainly, Hasidism has a history, a principle, an evolution, a literature, a folklore. But its strength lies in life, not in what could be its ideology. Baal Shem Tov does not only change thinking, but the climate and quality of Jewish existence.

Without him and his words, his songs, his disciples, and the power of his call, without the vertigo of the dance of thought and body, what would Judaism be?

Hasidism is not an exclusively "religious" phenomenon. It is a way of being, characterized by an increase in vitality and liveliness. Hasidism is the joy of living and the enthusiasm of realizing; it is the wonder of feeling the continuous vibration of the world, sensing that everything has meaning, that there is no "zone of indifference," that there is no wasted time.

Hasidism is, in reality, an opening to the world, to God, and to mankind.
Love for the Other, respect for his difference and his point of view.

Because Hasidism is neither a doctrine nor a set of petrified thoughts and gestures, it can oppose all dogmatisms and ideologies under which violence is perpetrated, resulting from human stupidity and malice.

Voltaire and Rousseau, Kant and Goethe, Mozart and Goya, Danton and Robespierre are all contemporaries of Baal Shem Tov.

But Music, Literature, Politics, and Philosophy, even when brought to their highest expression, did not prevent the deviation, the decline of Western man, and his fall into barbarism.
It is not God who dies in Auschwitz; it is man.
Hasidism is the critical vigilance against hatred.

It is not love for one's neighbor merely as a literary form. It is the encounter, the concrete face-to-face, where man learns to know the other man in order to respect him in his difference. For what is more homicidal than lies and ignorance?

Hasidism is not a senseless nostalgia.
"The observer, blinded by his prejudices, in his lazily schematic mind, will see in the Hasidic silhouette a castaway who absurdly clings to the raft of his past."
No, Hasidism is not an antiquity. It is true that thousands and even millions of Hasidim were killed, but Hasidism cannot be murdered.
Yes, it is true, the Hasidim of Bratslav entered the gas chambers singing: they proved, thus, in the heart of Hell, that they remained men until the end, that they did not allow themselves to be disfigured and humiliated by not dying before dying.

No, decisively, Hasidism is not an antiquity! It exists and must continue to exist to combat the force of prejudices and the ignorance we have of others, in which every word is a lie.

Here we will present themes and variations of this way of

being and thinking that, within Judaism, in a tradition that dates back to the Talmud and that blossomed more radically in Hasidism, has allowed and will continue to allow the fight against illusions, prejudices, and ideological stereotypes.

We adopt the categorical imperative of Adorno, which says: "To prevent Auschwitz from ever happening again is the demand of all education." Even though barbarism seems to be rooted in the very foundation of civilization, we must, above all, never lose hope of wanting to oppose it.

Adorno, however, thinks that "an awareness of the positive qualities possessed by the persecuted minorities would serve almost nothing." In a way, he is right, because minorities are not persecuted for their positive or negative qualities. Reason does not dictate the acts of madness.
Destructive madness merely disguises its violence with the garments of Reason.

But Rabbi Nahman of Bratslav taught us never to despair, even of man!
Man must return to himself to become aware and block the blind forces that drive him to suffer in every way.

Hasidism insists on teaching us critical vigilance to prevent man from playing the "power game" and bowing externally before the stronger one, a behavior that would tend to become the rule.

The meaning of Hasidism today?
Let us remember our future!

The urgency of the present, not a manic attitude that establishes memory as the primary value of our behavior.

Auschwitz is not just a place, it is a symptom and also a symbol: "the disaster of humanity"! Hasidism is the search, within Judaism, for what can destroy the "cause of Auschwitz."

Restoring to man his autonomy, the power to reflect, to self-determine, and to not play the game.

Where consciousness is mutilated, it bends over the body, and the sphere of the physical takes on the exterior form of an act of violence or linguistic gestures of controlled physical violence.

Hasidism is, thus, the set of modalities that allows each person to blossom, develop their abilities, and find the unique vocation they carry.

Hasidism is "expression"! It is joy and dance, expression of a happiness of living, it is also a manifestation of pain and anguish.

Telling one's pain and anguish, allowing oneself to truly experience the anguish that exists in the reality of the world, is also a fundamental way of developing a fullness of consciousness and thus avoiding most of the destructive effects of unspoken anguish, covered by false forgetting.

It is understandable why, for example, Rabbi Nahman of Bratslav advised his disciples to dedicate a moment every day to the possibility of crying and expressing their own misfortunes and hardships.

Hasidism is, through joy and pain, a fight against all forms of violence.

But Hasidism can become a movement and forget its vocation. In fact, "men who blindly insert themselves into the collectivity become something akin to inert matter, and they castrate themselves as self-determined individuals. This leads to a tendency to treat others as an amorphous mass."

But living Hasidism, aware of the violence that groups carry, highlights an ethic where the most important thing is not knowledge, but respect for each person's point of view. The ethics of Hasidism: make sure that inhumanity has no future! Hasidism came not only to understand man, but to transform him, to open the closed man to the other man, to the foreigner.

Thus, Hasidism proclaims the highest teaching of Abraham: Hesed, hospitality to the foreigner.

Hasidism sees in the Other, in his essential difference, everything that excites, stimulates, and agitates.

The Stranger is the miracle of novelty, which can, by his appearance, take an individual, or even an entire society, out of the mire.

By his appearance, the Stranger is the one who can help us become a taut bow, not a beaten and wilted branch.

For Hasidism, the Other makes the "event" possible; the Stranger is, therefore, the strange, the strangeness, the unknown that brings forth questioning.

The Other, in its absolute strangeness, is the discovery immediately called into question; it is the reborn uncertainty, the way in which the Other man can enter us without changing "the old knowledge of this world." Opening up to the Stranger is the possibility of questioning oneself, of giving a chance to the moment itself. The Hebrew says this wonderfully in a word that means, at the same time, "to invite" and "to create the occasion": lehazmine.

Hasidism is the consciousness called into question by the unique and singular point of view of the Other man. It is the refusal to see in a man the mere model identical to all other men.

Hasidism calls into question consciousness, not just the consciousness of the question posed.

The Hasid, the Hasidic man, thus experiences the loss of sovereign coincidence with himself, the loss of peace and complacency with oneself.

The experience of questioning continuously transforms the being of the Hasid, who becomes a question, a "man-question" and not just a man who has questions, who sits on questions.

As Edmond Jabès said: "The Jew does not rely only on questions: he himself becomes the question."

In refusing to fall into the "definitive" time and to preserve the grandeur of the "infinite" time, Hasidism places the emphasis on the word questioning, sets in motion the meaning against the dogmatism of Truth.

Hasidism renews, with questioning, the very foundation of Jewish thought, which dates back to the Talmudic period.

The fundamental interrogation, posed by Hasidism, does not presuppose the absence of an answer. It can exist, but it is necessary to distinguish between two categories of response.

To respond means to place oneself in a dynamic structure between the question and the answer.

The true answer, in its own formulation, reintroduces the question that originates it, that animates it: this is the living answer.

Hasidism cannot develop in the category of answers that refer only to resolved questions. This last form of answer wants to justify itself on its own, systematically, not as an answer, but as the result of judgments.

Judgment is the answer from which everything that constitutes it as an answer is evacuated, namely, its relationship with the very question. A judgment is an answer orphaned from its question.

The Hasidic answer contains within itself the power of the question, of life, and of time.

Hasidism has taught us, fundamentally, that "tradition is the noblest of freedoms for the generation that assumes it with a clear consciousness of its significance, but that it is also the most miserable slavery for one who receives it as an inheritance, out of simple spiritual laziness."

CHAPTER II
The Origins of Hasidism

Hasidism is a word that comes from the Hebrew hassid, which means "a person who carries hessèd." Hessèd, in the Bible, signifies a legal or moral bond between associated individuals. It is a sympathy spontaneously witnessed, without any prior association that would have made it natural or necessary between the two individuals.

Hasidism, in its modern sense, as we present it, is the last phase of the development of Jewish mysticism. It is a popular religious movement that developed among the Jewish masses of Poland and Russia from the early 18th century and persists even today.

In Jewish tradition, the word hassid and its plural hassidim, which can mean "pious" or "devoted," gave birth twice to a movement called "Hasidism." The first manifested in medieval Germany. The second is the Polish and Ukrainian movement of the 18th and 19th centuries, which has no strict relation to the first, except by name.

This work is primarily dedicated to modern Hasidism, which emerged in Volhynia in the first quarter of the 18th century.

There are several stories about Hasidism: some look down upon it, some celebrate it, and others ignore it. Some have seen it as essential to the dimension of a social revolution, while others view it as the rehabilitation of the imaginary and the dream. There are also those who see it as a vulgarization of the Kabbalah of Safed, from Rabbi Isaac Luria. It is all of these things at once, because Hasidism is not a single system, nor a single doctrine. It is a religious movement that has had numerous expressions, each focusing on one or another point in a privileged manner.

Birth of a Mysticism

To understand Hasidism as a new phase in Judaism, born in a specific time and place, it is necessary to analyze several parameters. This is what we will do in the following pages, studying the historical factors and the social and cultural environment of Eastern Europe in the years 1700-1750.

We said earlier, "Hasidism is the last phase of the development of Jewish mysticism." What does this mean?

The birth of mysticism, at a particular stage in religious history, is tied to certain conditions.

When great religions are born and established, they are not yet mystical religions. Initially, they are the result of social and religious situations that aim to place man in relation to God (or gods), and they allow man to assess the distance separating him from the world and from God. Religion is the "path" that helps man bridge the chasm that separates him from the Otherworld, which he calls God. Thus, the commandments, faith, and prayers are born.

Once the "path" is set in motion, the forces that led to the creation of religions continue to act. The aspiration, the need for transcendence, progress, and self-improvement arise, as if rooted in human personality, in the very soul of man. Thus, the force of religious creation continues to manifest and act, even after a particular religious system has been established.

Mysticism is born when new religious forces arise within the framework of a strongly institutionalized religion.

In reaction to the sedimentation of spirituality, in a community whose sensitivity has been atrophied, in a consciousness struck by a social disease, new forces begin to work.

The faithful then find themselves faced with an alternative:

either they seek to open themselves to a new path, in order to find an expression and a completely new historical context (this is what happened with Christianity; new religious aspirations led a certain number of believers to split from the traditional framework of the community of Israel); or, despite the new religious enthusiasm, they remain faithful to the traditional framework and try to stay within the community. It is then that mysticism develops, aiming at a reinterpretation of the data from the traditional religion, giving them a meaning in accordance with the new force that is about to reveal itself. As Sholem observed: "Mysticism has always existed in the history of religions, mysticism of a particular religion, and not mysticism for the sake of mysticism."

To understand mysticism, which is always a phase of development, it is necessary to look for the antecedents — or rather, to understand the transition from one period to another. Mysticism was not so much a stage of religious development, but the separation between one period and another. To put it another way, a mystical period is always a time of crisis, rupture, and breaking...

Thus, Hasidism is a time of renewal. Its founders and followers explode the medieval and ghetto inertia, aiming to put an end to the static Judaism that could only comment and was incapable of any initiative. In this revolution of mentalities, Hasidism proved to be a masterstroke. Contrary to the "emancipation" that began in the ghetto, through the disintegration and dissolution of Judaism, Hasidism led to emancipation not through escape from within, but in a much more powerful and warm Jewish integration. "In this sense, Hasidism is the precursor of all subsequent Jewish movements of renewal, stimulated by the spirit of the century, more rooted in the desire to be Jewish."

Hasidism "exists whenever a society realizes that it is not enough just to be, but that it is also necessary to exist, that to truly live, one must relentlessly seek new ways of existence, constantly continuing to reinvent oneself."

We must also raise the following question: what were the themes that truly played a determining role in the genesis of Hasidism?

Two realms of thought were modified in the old doctrines and ideas, contributing to a new worldview. The influence of Lurianic Kabbalah and the heretical theology of the Sabbateans. Here we are at an unavoidable crossroads in the history of ideas in modern Jewish thought. Nothing in it can be understood without understanding these two phenomena: the new Kabbalah of Safed and the rise of Shabbatai Tsevi and his satellite (which constitutes the story of Jacob Frank).

We will now explore the essential aspects of these elements necessary for understanding Hasidism.

CHAPTER III

"The Palace of Broken Vessels"
The Fundamental Themes of the New Kabbalah

Sholem established a fundamental distinction between the ancient and the new Kabbalah.

The primitive Kabbalah is the one that developed in Spain in the 12th century, giving rise to works such as the Zohar and the Book of Creation.

This tradition was concerned with the liberation from the chains of the chaos that is History: a quest to escape the confusion and catastrophes of History. The Spanish Kabbalists chose the path of what could be termed an archaeology, a retreat to the beginning, to the primal Genesis of the worlds. One could say that they sought individual redemption, a mysticism of the individual. The questions raised were: "What is the life of a Jew? What is the mystery of his existence? What is the secret of the Torah, of man's actions in this world, and his relationship with God?"

With the expulsion of the Jews from Spain in 1492, Kabbalah's focus shifted. The questions became more essential and anchored in reality, in historical reality.

The tragic and rather concrete experience of exile made exile and redemption vital issues for the spirits living and creating in the nation's religious domains.
This observation explains how a doctrine, emanating from a restricted circle, transforms into a collective movement, eventually becoming a historical factor of extraordinary power.

The new Kabbalists of Safed no longer concerned themselves with archaeology, but with the eschatology of the worlds, their end, and their redemption.

The new Kabbalah was Judaism's religious response to the expulsion of Jews from Spain.

In one generation, within the forty years following the expulsion, a fermentation and a messianic awakening of formidable power formed.

In the small village of Safed in Galilee, at this time, the greatest minds of world Jewry gathered.

It is here that Rabbi Isaac Luria elaborated and taught his vision of the world, which is one of the key moments in the history of Israelite thought. Luria was born in Jerusalem in 1534 and died in Safed in 1572 at the age of thirty-eight.

Rabbi Isaac Luria's Kabbalah immediately gained success because it answered the questions of existence.

It is necessary here to greatly simplify a set of concepts that were developed across thousands of pages.

The ideas developed by Rabbi Isaac Luria are, in fact, stages of a philosophy of history at a cosmic level. The Hasidic doctrine will later pick up these themes and give them an existential reach. There are three essential stages: Tzimtzum (or contraction), Shevirah (or breaking), and Tikkun (or repair).

Tzimtzum or Contraction

The theory of Tzimtzum represents one of the most surprising and bold conceptions in the history of Kabbalah. Tzimtzum originally means "concentration" or "contraction." In Kabbalistic terminology, it is better translated as "withdrawal" or "contraction."

Rabbi Isaac Luria posed the following questions:

How can there be a world if God is everywhere?

If God is the "All in All," how can things that are not God exist?

How can God create the world ex nihilo if nothingness does not exist?

Rabbi Isaac Luria responded by formulating the theory of Tzimtzum or "contraction." According to this theory, the first act of the Creator was not to reveal Himself to something external. Far from being a movement outward, or an externalization of His hidden identity, the first stage was a work, a withdrawal; God withdraws "from Himself to Himself," and by this act, He leaves an empty space within Himself, creating a place for the future world.

At some point, within the light of the Infinite (Ein Sof), the divine essence, or "light," eclipses; an empty space is left in the center. In relation to the Infinite, this space was nothing more than an infinitesimal point, but in relation to Creation, it was the entire cosmic space. God cannot manifest without having first withdrawn.

In Lurianic writings, the "empty space" is referred to by the term Tehirou. According to Luria, within this primordial void, a weak residue, a trace of divine fullness and light, remains, called Rechimu.

Shevirah or the Breaking

The second stage of the Creation process in Lurianic Kabbalah is called Shevirat Kelim or the "breaking of the vessels." After Tzimtzum, the divine light bursts into the empty space in the form of a straight ray. This light is called Adam Kadmon, meaning "primordial man." Adam Kadmon is nothing more than a first figure of divine light that emerges from the essence of the Ein Sof (Infinite) within the space of Tzimtzum, not in the entire space, but as a ray in one direction.

Initially, the emitted lights were balanced, meaning homogeneous (or yashar, or hozer). Later, the lights emanated from the eyes of the "primordial man" according to a principle of separation, atomized or point-like (olam haneqoudim). These lights were contained in solid vessels. When they later emanated, their impact was too strong for their containers, which, unable to contain them, burst.

Most of the released light returns to the higher source, but a certain number of "sparks" remain attached to the fragments of the broken vessels. These fragments, along with the "divine sparks" that adhered to them, "fell" into the empty space. At a certain point, they gave birth to the domain of qelipa, which is the "shell" or "crust," known in Kabbalistic terminology as the "Other Side."

The "breaking of the vessels" introduces a shift in Creation. Before the breaking, each element of the world occupied an appropriate and reserved place: after the breaking, everything is disordered. From then on, everything is imperfect and deficient, that is, "decayed" or "fallen." All things are, therefore, displaced from their rightful place, in exile... We insist on this fundamental aspect of Luria's explanation.

The key words here are "exile" and "sparks." The sparks of holiness fall into the world and are surrounded by shells that prevent them from being reached. Breaking these shells will be the work of man.

Exile is no longer just the exile of the people of Israel but, primarily, the exile of the divine Presence since the origin of the universe.

What happens in the world can only be the expression of this primordial and essential exile (it could be said: ontological). The fact that the divine presence, the Shekhina, is ontologically in exile is a revolutionary and bold idea. All the imperfection of the world is explained by this exile.

The historical importance of these ideas is evident. They provided an immediate response to the most important issue of the time: the existence of Israel in exile.

Luria's system gives Jews the certainty that they are not exiled just for their suffering, but that such suffering contains a profound mystery. Israel's bitter experience is nothing but a painful and concrete symbol of a conflict at the heart of creation.

This Kabbalistic explanation is of surprising originality, as it no longer considers exile merely as a test of faith, nor as punishment for transgressions, but, above all, as a mission.

We will show in detail that the objective of this mission is to elevate the scattered holy sparks and liberate the divine light and the holy souls from the domain of qelipa, which represents, on the terrestrial and historical level, tyranny and oppression.

Tikkun or the Repair

Tikkun, meaning "repair," "restoration," or "reintegration," is the process by which the ideal order is restored; it is the third fundamental phase of the great cycle proposed by Luria. The "breaking of the vessels" is an imperfection that requires repair; creation, both divine and human, must enter a process of Tikkun. It is necessary to restore things to their proper place and nature. Repair cannot be accomplished by itself; it is man who bears the responsibility for this stage. Man becomes responsible for the history of the world. Luria's philosophy of history thus becomes a philosophy of commitment, where man acquires a central place.
Man and God become partners in creation. It is true that, after the "breaking of the vessels," God revealed new lights and even began to repair the world, but this repair was not completed. The world, indeed, was not fully repaired by divine action.
The decisive act was entrusted to man.

One could say that the history of man is the history of Tikkun, or rather, the history of the failure of Tikkun.

Without this failure, history itself would not exist, and man would be in the situation of the philosopher concerning Hegel's "phenomenology of spirit" — he would be a finished being, that is, dead.

The "unhappy consciousness" that Hegel speaks of to describe the "Jewish consciousness" is precisely what defines its happiness, its fate, and its life.

The impossibility of achieving Tikkun, of obtaining repair, defines man as a "becoming" whose ethics is no longer that of perfection, but of perfectibility.

At the level of Rabbi Isaac Luria's texts, there is the idea of a first attempt at Tikkun in Adam Harishon, Adam the first man. Adam was supposed to repair the world but did not complete his task. Had he done so, Genesis would have immediately led to the messianic state, meaning there would have been no historical development. The cosmic exile would have ended, with Adam being the agent of redemption who would restore the world to its unity. The historical process would have been over before it even began.

Fortunately, Adam deviates. Instead of uniting what should be united and separating what should be separated, he separates what was united: "He separates the fruit from the tree."

The sin of the first man brings the world, which was almost repaired, back to its previous condition. What occurred after the "breaking of the vessels" is reproduced. The disturbances caused by the breaking of the vessels on the ontological plane were repeated and reproduced on the anthropological and psychological levels.

The entry of man into the Garden of Eden corresponds to the moment of the near-restoration of the breaking. The episode of the fruit and the exit from the garden signify the second break. The mission to repair and restore the worlds, which was Adam's, now falls on his descendants, but in an incomparably more difficult and complex way.

Before his sin, Adam understood in himself the totality of future human souls.
With the second break, the "sparks" of human souls shared, since then, the fate of the divine Shekhina, hidden in the scattered fragments of the broken vessels: they were imprisoned in the "shells" (qelipa).

Chapter IV
The Journey of the "Sparks"

The idea that the soul of Adam contains all future souls is revisited in the Midrash Tanhuma.

The key presented by the Midrash is the notion of each person's participation in the primordial adventures, which can be considered ontological, anthropological, and psychological givens.

Thus, Tsimtsoum, Chevira, and Tiqoun are not merely cosmological dimensions relegated to a mythical past, but relate to the human being, the humanity of the human being in general.

In addition to the nuances we will provide, this observation is fundamental to understanding the genesis of Hasidism. Rabbi Isaac Luria teaches that the soul is composed of 613 parts: each of these parts is, in turn, composed of 613 parts or "roots" (chorech); each of these "roots," called the greater ones, is subdivided into a number of smaller "roots" or "sparks" (nitsotsot).
Each of these "sparks" is an individual holy soul.
If Adam had completed his mission, all these souls and sparks would have remained in his embrace, and together they would have realized the restoration, the great Tiqoun.
Adam's sin completely ruined the possibility of this great Tiqoun. Some souls ascended to their root and will not return until the realization of Tiqoun. Other souls remained within Adam. The majority of the "soul-roots" and "soul-sparks" left Adam and fell into the realms of qelipa, the "shell," and formed, in the domain of the "Other Side," an "anti-Adam," the negative of the "Primordial Man," Adam-Qadmon, who resides in the realm of Holiness.
Man then enters the scene in History, participating in both Adam and anti-Adam, in the "side of Holiness" and the "Other Side."

The Elevation of the Sparks

In Luria's system, Tiqoun entails two operations: on the one hand, the gathering of the divine sparks, which fell along with the fragments of the broken vessels into the domain of the "shells" or qelipa; on the other hand, the gathering of the holy souls, imprisoned within the "shells" and subjected to the anti-Adam.

These two operations of Tiqoun are encapsulated in the symbol of the "elevation of the sparks."

This symbol expresses the true meaning and mystery of the history of humanity, and Israel in particular.

Some souls are sparks from the domain of Holiness, others come from the qelipa, the Other Side. The qelipa thus contains holy sparks awaiting their Tiqoun, the breaking of the "shell" that will liberate them. After Adam's expulsion from the Garden of Eden, each important moment in history is an opportunity for Tiqoun, but none of them leads to a radical advantage. The Kabbalistic reinterpretation of traditional texts, the Bible and Talmud, focuses on these privileged moments, their attempts, and their failures.

For example, the revelation of the Torah on Mount Sinai was a moment of Tiqoun: the world was on the verge of being completely restored, but the sin of the Golden Calf caused everything to return to a certain level of chaos.
It is important to note: the Law was given as a consequence of this new break, to effectuate a subsequent Tiqoun through the commandments. We draw attention to the 613 commandments, each one having the potential for the restoration of the 613 parts of the primordial Adam.

The Individual Sparks

In the previous pages, we spoke of sparks in a general and

collective sense. Here, we must emphasize the existence of "individual sparks," which constitute the particularity and uniqueness of each person. The human soul is composed of different lights or aspects, the sum of which produces the "individual spark" of each one.

Each "individual spark" is divided into three levels: nefech, rouach, nechama, and each level contains 613 parts.

An ascending hierarchy organizes the three types of soul, such that a person can only achieve a higher one after perfecting the previous one.

Two higher degrees, haya and yehida, are only attained by a few chosen souls who are illuminated by the highest of lights.

Man's task is to perfect his "individual spark" at all levels. It is possible that a single life will not be sufficient for this work. It is possible that Tiqoun must be realized laboriously and step by step, over the course of numerous lives and transmigrations, or Guilgoulim.

This idea of Guilgoul, transmigration, is the corollary of the theory of the "individual spark" and has penetrated the consciousness, or rather, the unconscious of Judaism. Strangely, this is an idea that was later rejected, though no less bizarre than the belief in a somewhat vague existence of the soul.

For the Kabbalists of Luria's school, it was important to discover the root of one's soul, as if only this knowledge would enable the person to restore their soul to its celestial root.

"It is the responsibility of each person to diligently seek to know the root of their soul, in order to perfect it and restore it to its original state, which is the essence of their being. The more a person perfects themselves, the closer they come to their true self."

It is important to note: there is an internal connection, a sort of sympathy between souls, which links all the sparks from the same root. They (and only they) can assist each other and influence one another in their shared Tiqoun.

Exile and Sparks

We have shown that Exile is the consequence of the break.
The question "Why exile?" is the one that generations of Jews
expelled from Spain and other countries asked.
The success of Luria's system largely comes from the fact (as
Sholem observed) that it provided an answer to the historical
confusions of its time.
Luria in fact proposes an explanatory system (a philosophical-
mystical thesis of the historical process).
Moreover, it is a thesis that takes man as the starting point,
holding him responsible for the destinies of the world and the
possibility of Redemption.
Man is responsible for History and also for understanding it in
its collective sense.
The entire people of Israel is vested with its own role. They
must prepare the world for Tiqoun, guide everything to its
rightful place; they have the duty to gather, to collect the
sparks scattered throughout the four corners of the world.
As a result, the people themselves must be in exile in the four
corners of the earth. Exile is not just an unfortunate event, but
a mission aimed at restoration and "selection."

In fact, restoration is achieved through a "separation" of
good from evil, aiming at an absolute distinction between
the domains of the Holy and the impure, which were mixed
during the original break and at the moment of the fruit
episode in the Garden of Eden.
The children of Israel are completely engaged in the process
of "elevation of the sparks," not only from the place where
they tread in exile, but also within the cosmic exile they have
been cast into internally and which they lead, in turn, little by
little, through their actions. It is from this conception that, we
repeat, the Hasidic masters created the theory and practice of
journeys, not initiatory, but that have impelled the "elevation
of the sparks

Chapter V
Creating the Messiah...

Rapidly, the ideas of Rabbi Isaac Luria captivated the imagination of the public. We argue that this fact is mainly due to the explanatory nature of his theory concerning the historical situation of the Jews of the time. Another factor to note is the concrete nature of the images proposed by Luria. The images are simple, even though the commentaries made on them are subtle and deep.

In the period we are analyzing here, the 17th century, Jews, whether rich or poor, lived in a constant sense of uncertainty. No one was safe from economic fluctuations and the adverse effects of political events. Because of this, there was no essential difference in the socio-psychological condition among the different communities of the diaspora.

In this context, the religious renewal in Safed and Lurian Kabbalah fulfilled an ideological function that significantly surpassed the simple religious objectives of its initiators.

The concrete images of Tsimtsoum, Chevira, and Tiqoun quickly took on a national dimension and a great dynamic power.

Tiqoun, emerging from its purely mystical and cosmic-ontological domain, soon acquired a political character, initially translated into the creation of a messianic tension. The "repair" of Tiqoun rapidly transformed into the "redemption" of both souls and bodies. Tiqoun was understood as the redemption of the individual and the collective.

The Role of the Messiah

As soon as the individual and the community have fulfilled their active role, symbolized by the "elevation of the sparks," Tiqoun will be completed: the "repair" will be finished, and all things will return to their original place in the primordial time of the world. This moment will be that of "redemption."

"Redemption comes by itself, for it is nothing else than the very 'Repair.'" The two notions are identical: if the world is repaired, it is impossible for "redemption" not to come, because it only expresses the perfect and flawless state of the world, a harmonious world where everything is in its place. This means that working for the "repair" of the world is the same as working for its "redemption." For Isaac Luria, the role we must play is to repair the world, both inwardly and outwardly, through our actions. This idea is one of the most fundamental, as it gives the Mitsvot (precepts of the Law, Halakha in Hebrew) cosmic significance and dimension. From here, there is a connection between traditional Judaism, its precepts, its ideas, and the mysterious fundamental forces that are acting in the entire world.

A person who fulfills a precept does not just fulfill it; they liberate a universal action. They repair something. The person's action becomes the very engine of history.
Through our actions, we are all engaged in a single messianic adventure, to which we are called to participate.
In this context, the Messiah is not the one who produces Redemption; he is the manifestation of the success of Redemption.
One can no longer wait for the Messiah; one must create him. As the symbol of the completion of Tiqoun, the Messiah loses his personal value, and it is understandable why he holds little importance in the Kabbalah of Rabbi Isaac Luria.
The notion of a messianic man disappears. There is no longer a savior who redeems humanity through his mere existence and suffering.
These notions are revolutionary in that they alter the ideas held about the Master, who was once seen as a miraculous savior who, by his actions alone, would bring about Redemption.
From Luria onwards, one no longer expects a determined messianic movement tied to a specially designated Messiah;

the Messiah becomes the entire people of Israel. It is the people of Israel, as a whole, that prepares to repair the original fracture. It is in this context that the Redemption of Israel (in the national and political sense of the term) was seen as a very real perspective.

To conclude the summary of the key concepts of the new Kabbalah, it can be said that its revolution precisely lies in restoring to the Jew the sense of their responsibility and dignity, making them aware that history is not a fatality, that the Jew is not predestined to be unhappy, but that, collectively and individually, they possess the means for a struggle for happiness and the forces for their freedom.

CHAPTER VI
The Deviations of Messianism
Shabbatai Tsevi and Jacob Frank

The expulsion of the Jews from Spain in 1492 was felt by the Jewish people as one of the most severe crises in their history after the fall of the Second Temple in 70 CE. We have shown that the new Kabbalah of Luria, in a way, provided an explanation and meaning for the Exile.

The year 1648 was eagerly awaited by numerous followers of the new Kabbalah, as they saw it as the year of final redemption. Contrary to expectations, the year 1648, in Hebrew the year 408 (Tah), was that of another great catastrophe for the Jewish people.

Poland was ravaged by ten years of war, attacked by the Cossack, Russian, and Swedish armies. The Jews of Poland were caught in this storm in a particularly dramatic way. In these ten years of war (1648-1658), more than three hundred communities were destroyed in Poland, and more than 250,000 Jews were killed. Those who survived were terrified and discouraged, performing the hardest and most humiliating work to avoid starving to death.

At this time, the unfortunate spectacle presented by the Jews expelled from Spain and Portugal was revived. Everywhere, one could see Polish Jews with gaunt and emaciated appearances, wandering in search of shelter. To the west, through the Vistula region, many of these fugitives reached Hamburg, emigrated to Amsterdam, or were sent to Frankfurt-sur-le-Main and other villages in the Rhineland. To the south, they sought refuge in Moravia, Bohemia, Austria, Hungary, and even Italy. Those captured by the Tatars were taken to the Turkish provinces and partly sent to the Barbarian States. In all the villages, they found a warm welcome among their co-religionists, who hurried to meet all their needs. In Italy, the communities imposed heavy sacrifices on themselves to ransom and help them; the wealthy members of the

Livorno community dedicated a quarter of their income to this charitable work. The Jews of Germany and Austria, nearly ruined by the Thirty Years' War, also pooled all their efforts to help them.

The massacres of 1648 are a fundamental event in the history of the Jewish people. One could even say, profound, in the same order as the expulsion of the Jews from Spain in 1492 and the destruction of the Temple of Jerusalem in 70 CE.

For contemporary consciousness, there is nothing comparable to the Shoah, the extermination of the Jews by the Nazis.

Judaism did not produce historiography. There is almost an allergy to writing about events. There are very few history books in it. Therefore, Judaism develops a historical consciousness through ritual, which becomes the bearer of the symbolic burden of history.

It can be shown that there are cultural traumas from profound events. The Exodus from Egypt was followed by the giving of the Torah, the destruction of the Temple gave rise to the creation of the Talmud, and the expulsion from Spain gave birth to the new Kabbalah of Safed.

One could assert that the massacres of 1648-1658 were of considerable importance, as they made possible the emergence of Shabbatai Tsevi and, later, Hasidism.

Shabbatai Tsevi

As we showed earlier, the figure of the Messiah in Luria's Kabbalah was collective. It is the people, as a whole, who constitute the Messiah. We had already emphasized this fact. However, in a situation of catastrophe as deep as the massacres of 1648-1658, the old conservative ideas about a personal Messiah — one incarnated in a person — reappeared and became stronger.

The question that hundreds of thousands of people had to ask themselves was undoubtedly: "Will the Messiah finally arrive?"

We fall back here into that vision where the Messiah inaugurates Redemption, whereas we emphasized that, in the new Kabbalah, it was Redemption that inaugurated the very possibility of the Messiah.

Seven years after the massacres, the Messiah arrives... His name is Shabbatai Tsevi.

Shabbatai Tsevi was born in Smyrna on April 9th (the commemorative day of the destruction of the First and Second Temples) in 1626 (5386). It was a Saturday.

Shabbatai Tsevi (Tsevi was his family name) was, in fact, a sick man, affected by a severe mental imbalance, oscillating between euphoria and ecstasy, anguish and melancholy, and going through successive manic-depressive states.

He was far from the traditional type of Messiah figure. He was not a conqueror who made the kings of this world tremble. He did not come to lead all things to their rightful place. He had a good rabbinical education, knew the Talmud, and was very versed in Kabbalah, particularly that of Luria.

One might ask, then, why he was considered such an important figure. His biography tells us that, in moments of religious exaltation, he would commit strange acts that consisted of violating the Law. In addition to deriving pleasure from these violations, he would engage in eccentric manifestations, declaring that through them, he was performing religious ceremonies with special meaning. Certainly, a mystical meaning at the level of Tiqoun. But the idea of a "holy transgressor," a "holy sinner," was not a messianic element supported by Jewish tradition.

These mystical-extatic acts of transgression did not allow

him to gain disciples. From his first appearance in Smyrna in 1648 until his proclamation as Messiah in Gaza (in 1665), he practically had no disciples to regard him as the Messiah. People laughed at him, declared him mad, or mocked him. However, a young rabbi who had come from the Talmudic schools of Jerusalem and settled in Gaza was not surprised to find him in strange circumstances.

Nathan of Gaza had studied the Talmud and the mysticism of the Kabbalah of his time with great devotion. He had a remarkable ability for imagination.

In March of 1665, he had a vision in which Shabbatai Tsevi (whom he had met on the streets of Jerusalem) appeared to him as the Messiah. Nathan convinced this much older man, torn by doubt and struggling against demons, that his mission was legitimate. Promoted to prophet of the Messiah, Nathan gave himself entirely to this cause, exhausting himself in multiple activities and sparking a great stir in messianism. In the eyes of the Jews of the diaspora, a prophet was to come to confirm the mission of the Messiah. Nathan of Gaza was received as this prophet.

The Events of the False Messiah

In a very short time, the movement gained the Jewish community of Yemen and spread from Persia to England, the Netherlands, Russia, and Poland. What the guardians of tradition had not foreseen, but what was perfectly understandable to the historian, occurred. When the expectation of the inauguration of the messianic era is preceded by a profound emotional experience, such as the massacres already mentioned, it can suddenly manifest itself to the consciousness of the masses, spreading with such force that it can survive on its own. However, disappointment was inevitable on the level of actual events. There had to be, necessarily, a contrast between the historical event and the religious experience, which was of a very different nature. The wave of enthusiasm that swept through the

Jewish communities for an entire year generated a spiritual movement that had not been foreseen by the rabbis and had not been seen in the ancient works.

If the movement had this considerable impact, it was because it came from Palestine. It was there that the prophet from Gaza recognized in the Kabbalist Shabbatai Tsevi, who was traveling from Smyrna to Jerusalem, the Messiah. Before this moment, no one had taken Shabbatai Tsevi's messianic claims seriously, as he had only expressed them intermittently. But Nathan of Gaza was convinced, from his own ecstatic experiences, of the legitimacy of Shabbatai Tsevi's claims. Over the course of a rather tumultuous year, from October 1665 to November 1666, a considerable number of people adhered to this messianic movement. These multiple factors then favored its development. There was an intense movement of penitence, which was considered a kind of final battle to bring about the time of messianic redemption. There was a vivid apocalyptic expectation, entirely born from the ancient texts and traditions, but it lost its literary and abstract character and suddenly took on a critical form. This brought to the memory of the Jews the warnings contained in these ancient texts.

The usual delaying attitudes changed when the passionate announcement that redemption was near took on the character of a mass movement. The emotion of the crowd accelerated what had been announced for future times and attributed it to the following day. For many people, the consummation of messianic redemption became, then, an interior reality before it was a historical reality. It is evident that a crisis had to occur on the day when it was realized that such a historical event, which had been announced, had not taken place.

Shabbatai Tsevi's personality exerted an extraordinary fascination, partly fueled by the aura of the marvelous and the legend in which he was quickly enveloped, due to the hope and credulity of the people. In the eyes of his closest disciples, he was certainly an ascetic and a mystic. In his moments of ecstasy, euphoria, or enthusiasm, he fulfilled his personal vocation by inciting people to transgress the religious law, presenting the type of "holy sinner" as a model for Judaism — an entirely exceptional figure until then. Sometimes, one can find in him the utopian vision of a renewed Judaism, under this anarchic form that has always been characteristic of messianism, and a declared tendency to perfect bizarre and grotesque rites that fulfilled certain roles in Jewish tradition, such as some festive rituals, though with their meanings inverted. Shabbatai Tsevi performed all these acts claiming a new messianic authority that was to surpass the measured and traditional authority of rabbinic Halakha.

The fervor reached a climax when, in early 1666, the Messiah arrived in Constantinople, where his followers awaited him to remove the crown from the Sultan's head and inaugurate the new messianic era. It is then understood why some Hebrew books that appeared at that time were marked with the seal: "First year of the renewal of prophecy and the Kingdom." The Turkish authorities detained the messianic claimant to the throne, but, to everyone's surprise, they did not condemn him to death. Instead, they imprisoned him near Gallipoli until September 1666. As a state prisoner, he obtained permission — no doubt through the bribery of some officials — to have his court. He would then receive delegations from all the countries that assured him of the support and adherence of the communities, particularly from the most important and influential centers of the Jewish world.

These incredible events left a deep impression on the faithful. The fast day of April 9th, which commemorates the destruction of the Temple, was declared, by messianic edict, the official day of the Messiah's birth and proclaimed a festival of joy. The enthusiasm knew no bounds, especially within Turkish Jewry.

The Fall of the Messiah

It was at the height of the movement that the catastrophe
occurred.

In September 1666, Shabbatai Tsevi was brought before the
Sultan in Edirne and presented with the following choices:
either maintain his messianic claims and suffer martyrdom, or
convert to Islam. He chose to deny Judaism.

The strength and depth of this messianic movement become
apparent in that this act of apostasy (the most scandalous
act imaginable for a faithful Jew) did not immediately, as
one might expect, lead to the collapse of the hopes that had
been raised. Other messianic movements within Judaism
throughout history had failed due to the disappointment
caused by the actual events, and did not leave any trace in the
consciousness of the chroniclers. But here, the transformative
power of this messianic movement was so strong that some
significant groups even came to accept the unprecedented
gesture of the Messiah. A gesture that had never been spoken
of or read about in the ancient Scriptures, and even less so
could be justified from these Scriptures.

The perplexity of the faithful was indescribable. The emotion
had been so vivid, so deeply ingrained in their hearts, that
the movement could not be extinguished by a mere feeling of
disappointment. Major groups of disciples decided to follow
Shabbatai Tsevi without leaving Judaism.

The "believers" (as Shabbatai Tsevi's disciples called
themselves) turned to the study of ancient works and
documents from the tradition.

For the theologians (or better, the ideologists) of the Shabbatai
movement, all the pages of the ancient books spoke only of
the necessary apostasy of the Messiah and the fulfillment
of his mission, under the figure of a transition or a descent
among the nations. They believed that the sparks of holiness,

scattered among the nations, had to be restored to their origin and that all things needed to return to their rightful place in order for redemption to be completed.

Nathan of Gaza, who had an exceptional ability to reinterpret ancient texts, was the first to conceive a new theory that pointed to a significant future. According to this theory, the messianic redemption of Israel from its exile had to follow a tragic dialectic in order to reach its consummation. The Messiah was to traverse all nations in order to fulfill the mystical mission of liberating and "raising" the sparks of holiness and the holy souls. To accomplish this mission, he could not be content with remaining in a world of holiness; it was not enough to bring the sparks of holiness out of the world of impurity. To complete his mission, it was necessary for him to penetrate into such a world himself. This explains why the Messiah was kept in a kind of exile, separated from his holy roots, in order to fulfill redemption.

This theory of Nathan of Gaza represented an unprecedented Jewish variant—and even a heretical one—of the ancient concept of the Descent to Hell. The apostasy of the Messiah became a necessary act for the success of his mystical mission, as well as for his historical mission. For Nathan of Gaza, the Messiah had not become Turkish; he had, in fact, remained Jewish. Only from his conversion did he live on two levels, one exoteric and the other esoteric, and until his return to the splendor of the messianic kingdom, these two levels would remain in contradiction with each other.

This theory adapted exceptionally well to the attitude Shabbatai Tsevi had taken. His double life, as a Muslim and a Jew, was accepted for several years by the Turkish government, which had initially expected a great deal from this eminent convert. As before, the Shabbatai "believers" continued to make pilgrimages to Edirne after the Messiah's conversion, and the messianic heresy expressed in the aforementioned theses quickly spread through a series of works that circulated in manuscripts. A kind of underground movement of Jewish messianism began, despite the understandable opposition and sometimes persecution from the official rabbinical authorities, reaching major centers and many regions of the diaspora.

Shabbatai Tsevi, after an exile in Albania, died in the autumn of 1676 in Dulcigno (Ulcinj). His death did not change the course of events: it was said that the Messiah was not truly "dead," but rather "engaged in a process of concealment." The doctrine of reincarnation, common among the Kabbalists, allowed for the possibility that the Messiah had appeared in successive forms from Adam until the most recent Messiah. By the 19th century, the Dönmeh (the followers of Shabbatai Tsevi) counted eighteen reincarnations of the soul of Adam and the Messiah throughout history.

There were different reactions among Shabbatai Tsevi's followers.

The "moderates" believed that the conversion and the "descent to hell" were the role of the Messiah, and only his. For them, as long as the last divine sparks (nitzotzot) of holiness and goodness, fallen after the primordial sin of Adam into the impure domain of the qlipot (i.e., the material forces of evil), were not reunited or restored to their source, redemption would not be completed. This was, therefore, the work left to the Redeemer, the holiest of all men. He must accomplish what the holiest souls of the past were unable to do: descend through the gates of impurity into the domain of the qlipot and save the divine sparks still imprisoned there. Once this task was completed, the Kingdom of evil would collapse by itself, for it could only stand because of the divine sparks within it. The Messiah was forced to commit "strange acts" (ma'asim zarim—a notion that would later play a central role in Shabbatai theology). Among these acts, his apostasy was the most shocking. Such acts were necessary for the completion of his mission.

This interpretation gave birth to a secret attitude that, viewed from the outside, might seem strictly rabbinic, but from the inside was specifically Shabbatai, or from a Jewish perspective, heretical.

The second reaction came from the "radicals." They raised the following questions:

Could one abandon the Messiah to his fate, just at the moment when he would be engaged in the most bitter phase of his battle with the power of the demon?
If all had experienced the redemption of the spark, why should this experience of the collective be different from that of the Redeemer? How can one explain that we should no longer wait for his aid?
A clamor was heard: "Should we not betray as he did? Let us descend with him into the abyss before its doors are closed again! Let us throw ourselves entirely, with the power of holiness, into the jaws of impurity, until a crack is heard from within!"

With Shabbatai Tsevi, they converted to Islam. The number of their "radical" disciples reached nearly two hundred families during his lifetime. Thus, it was noted that the majority of Shabbatai's followers remained outwardly Jewish, even though they believed in the legitimacy of Shabbatai Tsevi's mission.

Shabbateanism and Marranism

The new theory of the sparks, which implied the conversion of the Messiah and the radical "believers," was made possible by the existence of a Marrano mentality.

Let us remember that the Marranos were Spanish Jews who had converted to Christianity, outwardly practicing Catholicism while secretly (and covertly) continuing to practice Judaism.

Abraham Miguel Cardoso (1627-1706), who belonged to a

Marrano crypto-Jewish family from Spain and had officially returned to Judaism in Venice in 1648, explicitly says: "It was decreed that the King Messiah would wear Marrano clothing and thus become incognito among his Jewish brothers. In other words, it was decreed that he would make himself Marrano like me."

When one realizes that Cardoso was one of the most active proselytes of the Shabbatean movement, the significance of these words becomes clear. They undoubtedly reveal the hidden motivations behind the Shabbatean movement and shed light on almost all aspects of it. Underlying Shabbatean thought in its novelty was, above all, the deeply paradoxical religious sensitivity of the Marranos and their descendants, who constituted an important fraction of the Sephardic Jewish community. Had it not been for the psychology of these reconverted men, the new theology would never have found the fertile ground that allowed it to flourish as it did. Regardless of the true mentality of these first propagators, the Shabbatean doctrine of the Messiah was perfectly adapted to the needs of the Marrano mentality.

Thus, it can be said that the psychology of the "radical" Shabbateans was extremely paradoxical and "Marrano." Their guiding principle was essentially the following: the one who is truly as he appears would not know how to be a true "believer." In practice, this meant that:

The "true faith" cannot be a faith that men profess in public. On the contrary, the "true faith" must always remain hidden. Each individual has the duty to deny it outwardly, for it is like a seed planted in the bed of the soul that cannot grow without first being covered. For this reason, every Jew is called to become Marrano.

Just as a "true act" cannot be performed in public, in the eyes of all, so too the "true faith," the "true act," remains hidden, for it is only in secret that one can deny the falsehood of what is made explicit. Through an inversion of values, what was once sacred becomes profane, and what was profane becomes sacred. It is not enough to invent new mystical meditations (kavanot) to adapt to the changes of the times; a new type of action is necessary.

Before the coming of the Redeemer, the inner and the outer were in harmony, and it was possible to perform great tiqqunim through the outward observance of the commandments. But now, with the coming of the Redeemer, the inner and the outer are in opposition: the inner commandment, which alone could perform a tiqqun, has become synonymous with an external transgression. Bitoula shel Torah zehou qiyouma: "The violation of the Torah is now its true fulfillment."

The Fate of Shabbateanism

Shabbateanism took its first form in the "believers" who chose "voluntary Marranism" in the form of Islam. This sect, known as the Dunmeh (meaning "apostate" in Turkish), represented one of the first expressions of this movement.

The second form was that of the "moderate" believers, who outwardly remained traditional Jews in their external life but inwardly embraced the new Torah. Both groups existed in the Balkans and in Palestine. In the 18th century, the maaminim (meaning "believers") were concentrated in the north and east of Europe, particularly in areas like Podolia and neighboring villages such as Buczacz, Busk, Gliniany, Horodenka, Zholkiew, Tysmenieca, Nadworna, Phodaice, Rohatyn, and Satanow, but also in other countries, especially Romania, Hungary, and Moravia.

The Shabbateans who remained Jewish eventually played a key role in the transition from Shabbateanism to the birth of Hasidism.

The Final Tremor of Shabbateanism: Frankism
A final tremor of Shabbateanism must be addressed before

discussing Hasidism: the movement led by Jacob Frank.

Jacob Frank (1725-1791) is remembered as one of the most horrendous figures in Jewish history. Whether due to personal reasons or not, this religious leader behaved in every action as a thoroughly corrupt and degenerate character. It was to be expected that the Shabbatean movement, at the height of its contradictions and unexpected twists, would encounter a personality as strong as its own, one capable of extinguishing its last inner flame and perverting the final desires for truth and goodness that still animated the "believers" amid the ruins of their souls. Even if the doctrine of "sacred sin," or mitsya habaa baavéra (a commandment performed through a transgression), had already caused considerable damage, it is certain that a deeper shock followed when the "believers" encountered Frank himself. By then, they were already on shaky ground, where nothing could be considered impossible. Perhaps it was precisely this that attracted them to Frank. For Frank was a man unafraid to push everything to the extreme, on the verge of descending into the abyss, emptying the cup of desolation and destruction to the point where the last instinct of holiness became absurd. His followers, who were far from possessing the same abilities, were seduced by his audacity. Since neither belief in God nor fear of hell could deter him, they came to see him as the model of the true saint, a new Shabbatai Tsevi, God incarnate.

In 1759, a large number of Frank's followers converted with him to Catholicism. However, the majority of Frankists remained Jewish, living primarily in Bohemia and Moravia, with a significant presence also in Hungary and Romania.

Frank was a nihilist of rare authenticity. He was not an original speculative thinker, but he had the gift of finding the most striking formulas, the most eloquent examples, and the most concrete images. His aphorisms were compiled into a collection titled "The Sentences of the Lord" (written in Polish under the title Sliwa Panskie).

His doctrine practiced nothing but desolation. For this new prophet, it was necessary to liberate oneself from all laws, conventions, and religions. The authentic path consisted in eliminating every religious act and every positive belief. "I came into this world only to destroy and annihilate," he said.

Here is an essential element that will be found again as a foundation in Hasidism:

"To ascend, one must first descend," he would say.

"No one can climb a mountain without first standing at its foot. We must descend to the lowest level if we wish to ascend to infinity. Such is the mystical principle of Jacob's ladder, which I saw and which has the shape of a V."

"I did not come into this world for your elevation, but to cast you into the abyss. There is no further descent. We could not ascend from there with our own strength, for only the Lord can lift us from such depths with the power of His arm."

"Man will not be truly free until he is capable of living an anarchic life."

"In the place where we are going, there are no laws, for they were born from Death, and we are bound to Life."

Even more original was his proclamation:

"The Messiah will be a woman: 'A beautiful young woman without eyes.'"

Frank also had a "duty of silence," meaning the obligation to remain discreet about one's status as a "believer." Here, we find a new version of the original Shabbatean precept, that of not revealing one's true self. There is also the Marrano aspect that we encountered among the Shabbateans. Jacob Frank's conversion in 1759 represents another version of descending into hell in order to seek the sparks.

However, as Sholem emphasized, there is a positive side to the nihilism of Frank and his followers. Since the Frankists remained within the Jewish community and exercised influence there, their behavior raised the question of the impossible continuity of the conservative, medieval-type Jewish community, which was not only violently anachronistic in relation to external evolution but was also heading toward an internal collapse. Thus, one could agree with Mandel that the Frankists were the revolutionaries of the Jewish milieu and represented the avant-garde of what would later become the emancipated Judaism, rather than the continuity of the new Kabbalah of Safed, which followed the Shabbatean heresy and its numerous deviations.

It is during this same period that Hasidism emerges.

Chapter VII:
Baal Shem Tov - The Founder of Hasidism

At the moment when Jewish imagination was on the verge of exhaustion, and the spirit, in its quest for the impossible possibilities of Talmudic law, found itself at an impasse — especially given the deep scars left by the suffering of 1648 and the lingering winds of the messianic madness of Shabbateanism and Frankism — a miracle occurred. "Let there be light," and light appeared: Rabbi Israel ben Eliezer, known as Baal Shem Tov, the "Master of the Good Name," enters the scene of history. Modern Hasidism was about to begin its great march.

In the historical plan, Baal Shem Tov's personality remains vague, nebulous. Nothing can be stated with certainty about him. Those who claim to have known him or loved him can only speak of him as poets. They describe him as a dream.

Baal Shem Tov floats between myth and reality, between fiction, fable, and truth. He left no valuable autobiographical elements. "Obsessed with eternity, he neglects history and lets himself be carried away by legend."

Despite the legend, certain dates and facts remain with a more acceptable historical tone. Some place his birth around 1690, others in 1700, but all agree on the year of his death: 1760. He was born to elderly and poor parents in Okop, a small village in Podolia. Orphaned at an early age, he supported himself as a teacher's assistant. Hasidic tradition says that at the age of twenty, he retreated to the solitude of the Carpathian Mountains to engage in spiritual exercises and prepare for his vocation. Thus, he spent several years digging the earth, extracting clay that his wife would sell in the village.

At the age of thirty-six, he reappears as a spiritual master. Later, he settled in Medzhibozh, another small village in Podolia. It was here that he died in 1760.

However, one cannot believe, as legend suggests, that Baal Shem Tov (often abbreviated as Becht) came from nowhere. At this time, Eastern Europe was traversed by various semi-scholarly figures, thaumaturges, bone-setters, and preachers.

This "wandering intelligence," as Josef Weiss calls it, played a decisive role in the spread of the Shabbatean movement. Its members acted as reporters and transmitters, circulating new ideas faster than any form of publication. They stopped in every small village, particularly receptive to revolutionary ideas that could subvert the established order.

Baal Shem Tov was part of this subterranean intelligence. The expression refers to popular healers and magicians who traveled from village to village selling remedies and amulets. The medicines were mostly plant-based. It should be noted that the term "Baal Shem" was held in low esteem, even within this Bohemian fraternity. It was one of the lowest ranks, not comparable to the importance of a preacher, for instance.

During this period, the figure of the Tsadik Noded, the "wandering righteous one," predominated. Baal Shem Tov belonged to this Bohemian fellowship, always traveling, always bringing a new and good word.

These travelers explained their journeys in part as a way of gathering the sparks of holiness scattered throughout the world. Here, we begin to glimpse the connection between the Lurianic Kabbalah, Shabbateanism, and Hasidism. One could call this movement: "Journeys of a Spark."

Chapter VIII:
The Opposition to Hasidism

The first campaign of intimidation, slander, and repression against the dissident movement took place in the proud region of Lithuania, which developed and implemented it. The memories of the harmful consequences of the diffusion of the doctrines of the false Messiahs Shabbatai Tsevi and Jacob Frank in the 17th and 18th centuries were still fresh; these figures had also sought to liberate the Jews from very rigid laws and had emphasized mysticism and collective joy as paths to redemption. In this way, any idea or experience that did not come directly from a strict observance of Halakha (traditional law) was seen as heretical.

The Gaon of Vilna, who from the age of thirteen, after his Bar Mitzvah, lived in asceticism, secluded among his books and manuscripts, reaffirmed that a Jew could only claim their Judaism by obeying all the commandments of the Torah. He respected Maimonides as a brilliant codifier but not for his philosophical work. According to him, the laws had been given to be observed, period. It didn't matter to seek understanding or, even less, to change them. What was good for Moses and Rabbi Akiva should also be good for us. And now, a group was attempting to modify the code of life and the behavior of individuals and the community; here was a sect whose leaders allowed themselves to alter books, prayer times, and undermine the importance of Talmudic study, claiming that the recitation of Psalms was as valuable as the study of the Torah!

Reading the anti-Hasidic documents and pamphlets, one gets the impression that, beyond doctrinal issues, there was also the problem of customs: the actions and gestures of the Hasidim had to shock the sober and rigorous rationalists of Lithuania. The latter did not appreciate the spectacular exhibitionism of the Hasidim, who shouted in prayer, gestured wildly, beat on walls and pulpits to reach ecstasy.

Moreover, they gathered in private places, where they told bizarre stories and taught popular ways instead of studying the Bible. Worse, they drank a little, or a lot—let's say, quite a bit. The "respectable people" felt all of this was an outrage and cried out: blasphemy! Furthermore, this "sect" found some success, especially among disgruntled preachers and poor slaughterhouse workers. Oh, yes, the fortress had weak spots. Fissures appeared. Enough reasons for the notable persecutors and tempters to stop the wave.

The task of the opponents was so difficult that the Maggid of Mezeritch, the first successor of Baal Shem Tov, had the idea of sending his best emissaries to Lithuania. Nowhere could one find men of the stature of Rabbi Shneur Zalman of Lyadi, founder of Chabad. Together with his friend Rabbi Mendel of Vitebsk, he taught in White Russia, but his influence extended to Vilna. An unparalleled Talmudist and prodigious Kabbalist, he attracted young scholars who were intrigued by the movement. Even his worst enemies could not accuse him of ignorance. The notables had reasons to feel threatened and to act.

Another factor that exacerbated tensions was the diphtheria epidemic that ravaged the village of Vilna at this time; hundreds of children died. As usual, this was seen as a sign of punishment. Where punishment is mentioned, sin is understood. So who were the sinners? They were easily identified: members of the heretical faction, the Hasidim. Suddenly, they were blamed for every conceivable evil. Moreover, they had no respect for the Gaon, for his knowledge, and even for the Torah. They had to be punished. Some were publicly flogged, others expelled from the village. Hasidic meeting centers were dispersed, and their leaders were humiliated. It was decided to go even further with the repression, issuing mass excommunications against the Hasidim.

Communities near and far were mobilized against them. A

letter to this effect was signed by rabbis from Amsterdam, La Have, Metz, and Prague. The first excommunication ceremony (accompanied, according to the ritual, by the sound of the shofar and the light of black candles) took place after Passover in 1772; others followed, numerous in the large villages of Lithuania and White Russia. In the name of the Gaon of Vilna and other famous scholars, marriages with the "sectarians" were banned, as was sharing meals with them or maintaining any business relationships. The edict was read at fairs and all assemblies. It was war. A declared war.

The reaction to the work of Rabbi Yaakov Yosef, the first great ideologue of the movement, was violent. The Gaon of Vilna considered the work to be the height of insolence. With a medieval and quite monastic fanaticism, the Gaon immediately ordered, in all communities under his authority, the auto-da-fé of Toldot Yaakov Yosef. The scene of the auto-da-fé in the village of Brody has been described many times. From it, one mostly takes away the impression of a high degree of fanaticism from the Hasidism's opponents.

Over time, and thanks to the perseverance of great masters like Rabbi Shneur Zalman and Rabbi Nahman of Bratslav, the Hasidic teachings won over hearts and minds, and the quarrel deepened.

Rabbi Shneur Zalman was imprisoned in the St. Petersburg prison. The day of his release became a great victory for Hasidism. It is still celebrated today on the 19th of Kislev (in November or December) by his followers.

When we contemplate the situation of that time, we realize that the quarrel was not over. It resurfaced from time to time; excommunications and auto-da-fés were then quite harsh.

No, men did not become more generous or more intelligent! Intolerance, fanaticism, and stupidity are, unfortunately, still very present!

SECOND PART

THE DANCING WISDOM OF HASIDISM

The boy observed the old man dancing, and it seemed as though he danced for eternity.

Grandpa, why do you dance like this?
Learn, my son, man is like a spinning top.
His dignity, his nobility, and his balance, can only be attained through movement... Man is made and unmade, never forget this!

CHAPTER I

The vowels of desire
An ethics of action and words

We have insisted quite a bit in this essay on the metaphor of sparks, first addressed in Luria's Kabbalah, and later in Shabateanism. Now, we must examine the form that these sparks, and more particularly "the elevation of the sparks," have taken in Hasidism.
The mutation of the concept lies mainly in the transition from the collective to the individual, from collective responsibility to individual responsibility in relation to the more intimate everyday life and everything that surrounds it. Every man becomes the redeemer of a world that is his; he directs it, and only he must direct it. He proves what only he can prove.

No one can accomplish the work of another, no one can elevate a spark that is not their own.
It is this personalization of the sparks that constitutes the great Hasidic revolution. Man steps out of the collective mass of the institution to become a "subject" in the true sense of the word.

Baal Shem Tov and his disciples insist on the mystical connections between man and his environment.

58

Each person must seek bonds containing sparks drawn from the root of their own soul in order to free them.

In other words, the mutation from Luria's Kabbalah to Hasidic doctrine is the transition from the ontological-metaphysical plane to the psychological and personal plane.
Hasidic texts hesitate on one point of this theory: Is the elevation of personal sparks the work of every man, or only of the tzadik (righteous one)? In general, it can be said that the dilemma lies within the domain of Hasidic doctrine. It seems that this is still the case today. Personally, we choose the path that gives each individual the opportunity to build their own path and rediscover their own sparks.
In any case, the new understanding of the elevation of sparks has profoundly marked Hasidism on various levels. In particular, concerning texts and study. The sparks are present in everything, without exception. There is, therefore, no place or sector that can be called profane in contrast to the specific domains of holiness.

Man always has the opportunity and even the obligation to elevate sparks, but the forgetfulness of his responsibility always threatens him. An awakened consciousness can discover the "spark" in every domain of life and, thus, seek in the world a higher and more fruitful meaning.
This worldview has nothing to do with pantheism but rather with a way of seeing it always from a new perspective. In this way, simple and insignificant actions become fundamental.

Here, there is almost a phenomenological attitude towards the letter, a return to things in themselves, a return to the concrete and to existence.

The return to existence is not one of crude or simple materialism, but a renewal of transcendence in man. Rediscovering the sparks in everything means seeking the absolute that escapes us but creates a distance, a desire, a question, and a movement toward the beyond, which is precisely the life of existence in its etymological sense, the capacity to leave oneself, to surpass oneself, and to engage in a creative movement. It is there that man must make the hidden life of the absolute shine.

This "there" is not merely the destruction of past worlds. It means, more deeply, the return of transcendence to the interior of the world itself. There is an existential impression of sacred sparks in all things.

This means that the sparks are opened in the time of fertility and creativity.

To elevate the sparks means to live a fuller life. We will show in the following pages different facets of the elevation of sparks. The sparks will underlie all the proposals that follow. We will try to show throughout this work that Hasidism insists on placing each person's responsibility in relation to their own history.
Hasidism presents an ethics.

Ethics is not just a word, but a movement, a search, a break. There is ethics when there is "the search for a place where the word sets into motion its points of renewal, where everything is supposedly acquired, beginning with the language in which it bathes, a heritage that should make return... in a circle." The word, the language, and speech are not taken here in their purely linguistic sense; they denote the whole set of signs in the world, the body, society, in short, everything that organizes to signify something. Thus, we can speak of an ethics of the word, of action, of knowledge.

Action, birth, and freedom

For Hasidism, the ethics of action means that there is a way of proceeding that corresponds to the human capacity to begin, to undertake, to take initiative. Ethical action opposes behavior, which is nothing but a repeated gesture imitating a gesture already made, without the force of innovation.

Hasidic ethics is the interruption of the flow of life that leads to death; it is the capacity to start anew. Let us always remember that men, even though they must die, are not born to die but to innovate.

Hasidic action is a birth, opposed to the gesture of repetition; it insists that man is a new principle, an initiator.

Ethics is thus linked to the concept of "natality." Man can have an ethical action because he is a "being-for-birth." The very ability to begin has its root in natality because the human being appears by virtue of birth.

We reject here what the Talmud calls Pidyon HaBen (the redemption of the son), which means that the firstborn son does not belong immediately to his parents. For thirty symbolic days, the child belongs to the Cohen, to the priest. The father must redeem his firstborn—an act that reverberates on all children. Biological ties imply no ownership: the father, the mother, and the child must become aware of birth, not as a continuity, but as a rupture.
There is the need to feel like a creature.

To be born, to be a creature, are two essential concepts for the very existence of ethics. In the history of ideas, one can understand in this way the fundamental meaning of the discussion between Aristotle and Maimonides about the creation or non-creation of the world.

Hasidic action views the world not as it is, but as it can be. The creation of the world and of man gives rise to a world and a man who are not the whole. Ethics resides in this "non-being-the-whole." The perfection of man is not the "total-being" but the "not-yet" of total-being.
In a formula used by André Neher, one can say that "the perfection of man is his perfectibility." By virtue of his placement in the world, man is liberated, and therefore within him is the promise of a "becoming."

This ethics of action implies taking a stand concerning the principle of reason and the philosophy of history.

Indeed, for there to be ethical action, that is, a gesture founded on novelty, it is necessary that history not be reduced to the mere tracing of a pre-established rational order.

Ethical action is based on the perspective of a radical change and excludes a causalist theory. It faces novelty without yielding to the vertigo of the identical.

The vowels of desire

The Hasidic action we have just described is a corollary of a modality of the word, which is equally called ethics.
The Hasidic word is an ethics of the word. The ethics of the word is the refusal of the established word, dead over time under the feet of its insignificance. The ethics of the word, the ethical word, is the putting into motion of speech against what has already been said.
Ethics is also break, fracture, fissure. It is, first of all, the shattering of the word into its letters, underlining that the relationship between vowels and consonants is not self-evident and that it is necessary to introduce Desire into it. The ethical word is not the one transmitted by inheritance; it is not the old or the new testament, it is not the announced word, nor the announcer or the realizable. It does not wish to accumulate anything. On the contrary, it introduces the white space, the interval, the distance. It is murmuring, like Moses' word and the hesitant sound of the shofar.

The Hasidic word is laughter, dance, and play. It opens the word by itself; it opposes the pre-fabricated language of concept, cliché, advertisement, and politics. It is against the "we-all-say-the-same-thing-together."

It is a word through which the subject is constructed (and "deconstructed"); in which he is present (even without knowing it), which means that a word from the realm of the unconscious is fundamentally ethical inasmuch as it sets into motion, or shakes, what has already been spoken.

The Hasidic word is not, therefore, the word of the Book around which the group gathers to form a collective being. The Hasidic word is, on the contrary, the one that allows for the reversal of the group, enabling it to gather around this reversal.

The group, that is, the "we" of the discourse of total administration, of the closed discourse, seeks to suppress all differences, all singularities, all oppositions.

The Hasidic word is the one that escapes the suppression of differences.

CHAPTER II

For an Existential Word

The ethics of Hasidism proposes a set of processes that allow one to free oneself from the forms instituted by experience, in order to invent new ways of life.
The different actions of man should attempt to invent new forms of experience never before established. Such an ethics is not an abstract duty, but a way of life choice.

The Hasidic man is the man of hidush, of novelty. For this reason, ethics is connected to hermeneutics; the latter is not only understood as the experience of semantic comprehension, but embodies a fundamentally existential attitude, making it possible to invent oneself. Hasidic ethics asserts that each person has the duty to seek freedom to invent other forms of experience.

This ethics does not equate freedom with the discovery of any truth or authenticity, but rather with a constant effort of liberation and self-invention.

The hidush man exists when he ensures that each day is not a repetition of the one that preceded it. In Rabbi Nahman's language, this translates to the "prohibition of being old." Talmudic ethics is a demand for the unrepeatable.

Historically, Hasidism has revealed itself as a critique of the official rabbinic institution of the time. This critique can extend to all institutions in general.
But what Hasidism has most raised is the democratization of study, the possibility for everyone to have access to interpretation.

This subjective relationship with texts already existed in Talmudic tradition, but study was reserved for an elite. Thought became dogmatic, ideological.

The Hasidic mutation can be seen in this small story, which can be considered a paradigm of the cultural and existential revolution prompted by Hasidism.

A disciple came to see his Master, who asked him, "What have you learned?"
The disciple replied, "I have read the Talmud three times."
The Master said, "But what has the Talmud taught you?"
Hasidism gave study all its subjective and existential dimension.
To understand the existential dimension of study introduced by Hasidism, it must be compared to another approach we call the historical approach. This can be found in history both before and after Hasidism. But Hasidism opened a new path that became impossible to ignore.

Hasidism performs what could be called a Copernican revolution, in the same sense as the critical philosophy understands it: a revolution in method, in relation to things. Instead of seeking the most general properties of being, as in traditional ontology, it aims to rediscover man, who is forgotten under the weight of objects and their truths. Classic study, as developed and imposed by a certain current, transformed the text, the Torah, and the Talmud into mere objects of technical, even mathematical, exploration, excluding from its horizon the concrete world of life. The more the pre-Hasidic man advanced in his knowledge, the more he lost sight of himself and the world, drowning in the forgetfulness of man and the "human vision."

What we call the objective historical method, or scientific method, is one that is undertaken in view of knowledge, which aims to understand the text or texts.

Hasidism seeks to understand man. For it, "to understand a text is, first and foremost, to understand oneself before the text."

By insisting further on the historical method of texts, the

counterpoint with the existential search will be even more eloquent.

a) The Historical Approach to Texts is the method that considers the past as belonging definitively to History. The past becomes intelligible only after the wise and critical mediation of the historian. In this instance, texts acquire a mythical dimension and are considered as a "mythogenic entanglement of survival" that the sage tries to decipher. It seeks to find, reconstruct, understand the life of Hebrews in the desert, the life of Jews in the Talmudic period, etc. It shows how Jewish language, clothing, and habitat were borrowed from the Greek and Roman worlds. The philologist finds his sweetness in deciphering words with Persian, Greek, or Latin consonances, which allows him to bring to light the similarities or differences in customs, mentality, and myths.

Despite this will and effort to know the texts and traditions, the historian maintains his limits; in other words, he makes the past remain past and the present, present. The historical method consists in objectifying tradition and methodically eliminating any influence that the present, in which the historian lives, might exert on the understanding of the past.

The interpreter-historian approaches his object of study with a precise rule: "Only one who knows how to stay out of the game can understand."

To whom are the texts of Tradition addressed? For the historian, the answer to this question is very simple: to everyone, except to him. By following this way of interpreting the methodology of human sciences, it can be said that the interpreter imagines a recipient for every text, whether expressly designated by the text or not. The recipient is, in all cases, the target reader, with whom the interpreter tries not to confuse himself. It is impossible for the historian to conceive of himself as the recipient of the text, submitting to the demand of the text.

The historian works from the following hypotheses: it is necessary to transport oneself into the spirit of the time, think according to its concepts, according to its representations, and not according to one's own era, to reach, in this way, historical objectivity. All this amounts to saying that temporal distance is an obstacle to understanding: objective understanding. Or, paradoxically: this temporal distance is precisely what makes the historical situation of interpretation possible. Objective knowledge could not be achieved except on the basis of a certain historical distance. However, even if this distancing of the object conditions a certain objectivity and a certain positivity in research, the entire negative aspect of the historical method would arise, in fact, from the tacit hypothesis that would state: a thing does not become objectively known in its lasting significance unless it belongs to a well-defined context. In other words, as soon as it is dead, it becomes of historical interest...

b) The Existential Approach, however, does not consider any temporal distance separating the interpreter from the text.

One might cite, in support of this approach, the famous text from the Midrash that comments on verse 15 of chapter 29 of Deuteronomy: "It is not only with you that I am concluding this covenant and this pact with imprecation, but also with him who is here with us today before our God... and with him who is not here with us today."
All those who would be born in the future, until the end of all generations, were present with them on Mount Sinai (Pirqué de Rabbi Eliézer, Chapter 41).

The existential attitude is based on the idea that each era must understand the text transmitted in its own way. The true meaning of a text, as it is addressed to the interpreter, does not depend on these occasional factors represented by the author and his target audience.

Thus, one can state that the meaning of a text – if it is a great text – surpasses its author, not occasionally, but always: that is why understanding is not merely a reproductive attitude, but always also a productive attitude.

The existential approach does not aim to understand better, but to understand differently. In this framework, temporal distance must be considered as a positive and productive possibility given to understanding. "It is not, therefore, an abyss opened, but passed through thanks to the continuity of origin and transmission, in the light of which all tradition offers itself to our eyes."

The existential approach rests on the personal implication of the interpreter in the event of comprehension. The interpreter is literally "between-held" by the text he comments on and understands; his own ideas are, from the outset, implicated in the revival of the meaning of the text; his personal horizon becomes decisive. But he does not interpret from a personal point of view that remains or imposes itself, but rather as an opinion or a possibility of engaging in the game, which is put into play and helps in a true appropriation of what is said in the text.

The reader-translator-interpreter, existentially confronted with the texts, does not, in the first instance, seek to go back to a past life, to a past meaning. His "understanding" means participating in what is being said in the present. The subjective interpretation precedes the comprehension itself.

In fact, it is not the text that is understood, but the reader. He understands himself. Understanding a text is, first and foremost, applying it to oneself. But this application does not limit the text, because we know that the text can and must always be understood differently.

CHAPTER III
The Tsimtsoum of the Spirit

The "Manifesto" of Rabbi Nahman of Braslav

For Hasidism, the first attitude towards tradition is contestation. Contestation allows opposition to the transmission of stereotypes characteristic of ideological discourses.

Hasidism does not accept that the word of a text be heard through the prison of a maintained and sedimented discourse. This explains why Rabbi Nahman of Braslav (1772–1810) once boldly stated such radical propositions as the following:

"There are rabbinic masters reputed for their knowledge of the Torah. They have extensive knowledge of the texts and interpretations given by their predecessors. But precisely because of this, they are unable to innovate (lehadèch) in the Torah, for they are too wise. As soon as one of these masters tries to innovate something, his vast knowledge immediately disturbs and imprisons him; he begins to formulate numerous preliminaries to summarize the synthesis of his knowledge on the subject, and in doing so, his own words become confused, and he cannot pronounce any new, interesting word.

When someone desires to invent new words (with new meanings), they must restrict their knowledge (literally: make a Tsimtsoum in their spirit), that is, they must produce the void, not rush into familiar preliminary considerations that confuse their spirit and are unnecessary for innovation. They must act as if they do not know, and only then can they invent new meanings progressively.

To those who wish to innovate meanings in the Torah, it is permitted to innovate and interpret everything they desire, everything they can innovate with their spirit, on the condition that they do not invent new laws.

It is also permitted to innovate even in the domain of the Kabbalah of R.I. Luria according to their possibilities, as long as they do not invent new laws."

In fact, for Hasidism – and Rabbi Nahman is one of its most paradigmatic figures – man does not only have the right to innovate, he has the duty to do so.

Innovate or die, that is the motto.

In the text from Sihot Haran we quoted earlier, Rabbi Nahman proposes, on the one hand, a methodology that allows access to the new word, and, on the other hand, a violent critique of the masters (here understood as those who think they possess mastery over their own word and the word of others).

The method is well known; we are not far from the docta ignorantia; it is the "not knowing", a consequence of a Tsimtsoum of the spirit. Man must withdraw from "self" in order to access himself.

The first "self" is not truly "self"; it was constructed, pre-fabricated by institutions. The subject is always and primarily, the product of institutional pre-fabrication: "pre-fabricated subjectivity". And when the individual begins to speak, they do not speak: they are spoken.

Here arises a fundamental question: is it possible to escape from this situation? Can one exit the pre-fabricated subjectivity, these "prêt-à-parler" discourses for everyone and no one? The "prêt-à-parler" discourse is the discourse of institutions and of public opinion. This is understandable, for the vocation of the institution – sometimes an unconscious vocation – is to create opinion and therefore, the non-word and the non-thought.

A social capture of subjectivity is established here. This means that being and text maintain deep and fundamental relationships. It means that "subjectivity is, in principle, this:

we are born to incarnate a certain ideality, a juridical ideality, of the human subject as a living exemplar, and to incarnate images in the reproduction of this particular kind of images that are texts, through which we cast our identity into the social descent of truth."

If being is being according to the text (institutions), according to the opinion linked to the environment where everything that is said has already been said, continues to be said, and never ceases to be said, then "to be or not to be" no longer makes a difference, because in any case, one is not, but simply "has been".

If man is thrown into the impersonal being of the social or religious institution (for Rabbi Nahman, in the words of infallible masters in their mastery) and it is impossible for him to bring forth his own world, the question of being no longer matters (that is, for the defenders of this ideology). In this conception, man was born before birth (meaningless birth).

Everything we have just said can be framed within what could be called a philosophy of Totality and the Neuter.

It is against this totalitarian philosophy of totality and neutrality (neutralization of the subject) that Rabbi Nahman and Hasidism in general oppose.

Hasidism aims to oppose the capture of subjectivity by society, opposing texts that model by annihilating the existence of the subject.

A Deconstructive Practice

Thus, the essential heritage of Hasidism is a deconstructive practice of language and thought.

Rabbi Nahman of Braslav states in another text:

"Even a simple man, if he has time to read, and observes the letters of the Torah, will be able to see new things, with new meanings, that is, through intensive observation of the letters, like those that began to 'make light', to combine (cf. Yoma 73b), he will be able to see new arrangements of letters, new words, and will also be able to see in the book things that the author had not thought of. And all of this is possible even for the simple man, effortlessly... Therefore, it is not necessary to intentionally rehearse for this experience, and it is possible that, precisely by rehearsing, he will not see anything, since all this also pertains to the simple man."

What Rabbi Nahman means is that every text goes beyond itself, its power-to-say surpasses its intention-to-say; to adhere to what a text intends to say is to pass by the transcendental dimension that exalts it. Every great text is the place of a particular creation, of an original thought that brings forth something that could not have existed before.

"This creation cannot proceed without breaking, a fragmentation. Our true contribution to such a text and to the thought it enunciates can only aim at finding this moment of creative fragmentation, this different and renewed dawn where, suddenly, things take on another aspect in the unknown landscape.

This implies that, for us, the text of the past and the thought it contains become new beings in a new horizon, which we create as objects of our thought in a different relationship with its inexhaustible being."

That is why, in a certain way, no "faithful" reading is ever truly important, and no important reading is ever truly "faithful".

Reading, an Act of Freedom

For Hasidism, study is an act of resistance to "the language of institutions". This resistance, a true combat, reopens the terms to their polysemic possibilities. Everything takes place in the rupture, in this act of "de-signification". The unique, univocal, and monossemic language of the institution, being the foundation of its totalitarianism, its intolerance and violence, is important so that, through the act of "de-signification", the subject and their word access or reaccess freedom.

It is also very significant that the festival of Passover (Pesach), the time of transmission to the children (and also the opening of the new year), is based on the transmission of the subversive capacity of language. Transmitting freedom involves the possibility of a subversive reading of the fundamental texts. Freedom passes through the possibility of escaping the "engraving" of the Law on the Stone Tablets: Al Tiqra Harout ela Hérout – "Do not read 'engraved' but 'freedom'".

When Rabbi Nahman often insists on this point: "on the condition that new laws are not invented", it does not mean that the novelty of the law disorients it, but that this law, when it comes to join the others, reinforces the institutional word. The supplementary law is rejected because it strengthens the institution and the guardians of its ideology, rather than weakening and destroying them. The man, continuously building himself, has no possible future except in the tireless succession of making and unmaking meaning, reading and "de-reading" the text. The rule of interpretation is clear. It does not occur through repetition, by paraphrasing the base text, but literally by detaching, by going "Beyond the Verse", by passing from the other's text to one's own text. Through this creative reading, the reader is truly born; after a biological birth, followed by a legal – institutional and social – birth, the subject is born as a differentiated individual. There is the passage from a "text without a subject" to a "text with a subject". Rabbi Nahman's manifesto of contestation through his text Sihot Haran (No. 267), which could be entitled "A Small Manifesto for the Right to Subjectivity", is a political manifesto.

Through this manifesto, the Law and its commentaries are no

longer inspired words, belonging only to a few mouths, but democratic words belonging to every human being.

CHAPTER IV
The Wisdom of Uncertainty
The Importance of Each One

The right and the duty to innovate, which has just been emphasized, clearly show the place of the individual and the concrete person.
One of the key ideas of Hasidism is the responsibility entrusted to each person.

Through innovation, man constructs himself and, in doing so, opposes the danger of preconceived thoughts; moreover, as the new interpretation is his own, he becomes consciously responsible for the individual and collective path he must build.

"It is understood, then, that for Hasidism, each person born into this world represents something new, something that did not exist before, something original and unique. It is the duty of every person in Israel to recognize that by their particular character, they are unique in this world and that no one like them has ever existed, because if someone like them had existed, there would be no need for them to be in the world. Every man, taken individually, is a new creation in the world, and is called to fulfill his particularity in it. The first task of every man is to actualize his unique, unprecedented, and never-before-repeated possibilities, not to repeat something that another, even the greatest of all, has already done. This idea is expressed by Rabbi Zousya shortly before his death: 'In the other world, they will not ask me: Why were you not Moses? They will ask me: Why were you not Zousya?'" (Martin Buber)

This text by Martin Buber echoes that of Emmanuel Lévinas: "The personal—subjective—relationship to the text, the 'Revelation' as an appeal to the unique in me, this is the specific meaning of the meaning of Revelation. Everything happens as if the multiplicity of people—the very sense of the personal—holds the condition for the fullness of 'absolute truth', as if each person, by their uniqueness, ensures the revelation of a unique aspect of the truth, and if certain people were absent from humanity, some aspects of the truth would never be revealed. This suggests that the totality of the true is made through the contribution of many people: the uniqueness of each ear carrying the secret of the text, the voice of Revelation, as inflected by each one's ear, is necessary for the Whole of Truth."

This same idea is expressed in Hasidic texts, formulated in this way: each person is a letter or part of a letter. The book is fully written when no letter is missing from it. Each person has the obligation to write their letter, to write themselves, that is, to create themselves by renewing the meaning, their meaning.

We have insisted on the fact that understanding and interpreting are inextricably intertwined; there is an existential critique here concerning the historical approach to texts. The interpreter-historian is mistaken when they believe they eliminate or exclude all subjective participation from understanding. In fact, "historical thinking always contains, from the start, a mediation between these principles (understanding and interpreting) and personal thought. To try to avoid one's own concepts in interpretation is not only impossible but manifestly absurd. Interpretation is precisely to engage one's own prior concepts."

Here is a brief passage from Maimonides in his introduction to the commentary on Merkava ("The Chariot"), one of the parts of Jewish thought where the objectivity of knowledge, interpretation, tradition, and transmission could have been discounted.

"What I believe to possess as mine goes no further than a mere conjecture and a personal opinion. There is nothing in the context of divine revelation that has made me know what it truly intends to say, and what I have concluded from the content of this divine revelation I have not learned from any teacher, but from the texts of the prophetic books and the discourses of the scholars, as well as the speculative propositions I possess, which have led me to believe that this is so. However, it is possible that it is different, and that something totally different was intended."

The purpose of this quote is not to deny the existence of "inspiration" but to suggest that "inspiration would lie in the exercise of reason itself. Thus, logos would be prophetic!"

Based on the above, the commentator can engage with their whole personality, their experiences, their readings — summarizing, with all their will. Commentary is not a disconnected text, nor an orphan text.

It is also necessary to be wary of the objectivist or pseudo-objectivist will that, preferentially, unveils a way of marginalizing, in a negative sense, the meaning of the text. The commentator, despite their refusal, inevitably intervenes much more than they say or believe.

Thus, it may be necessary to first affirm one's way of walking, rather than pretend to attain the illusory perfect transparency of the ideal commentator. One must refuse to claim an invisibility "that would allow one to discover the work in its truth"... Commentary does not come second, after a so-called first text, at least to the extent that it seeks to "repeat a path that, in fact, had never been carried out."

Even if it is merely repeated, the commentary is already different.

"In repetition, what is said enters into this essential difference."

The Search for Meaning, Not Truth

In his quest, the Hasidic man doubts. He does not seek truth, but meaning. The question is not: "How did God create the world?" but, "Since the text tells me that God created the world, what does this mean for me?"

The Hasidic man is always in motion, moving from certainty into the uncertainty of the "not knowing" that Rabbi Nahman spoke of.

He is essentially a "seeker," and his work is essentially a "search." With Rabbi Nahman, we find the end of "belief" (written here in quotes so as not to confuse it with common faith).

For the Hasidic man, there are always battles to fight, possibilities of flaws to be glimpsed. Situations to choose without rest. The Hasidic man does not know external certainty, always comfortable. In the "belief" that turns into "search," there is always a "pro" and a "contra," and as soon as one chooses the "pro," one is well aware that doubt can articulate the "contra."
The "search" or "belief" is a paradox: the assumption of "there is" and "there is not" at the same time; a hyperdialectic of an infinite tension between two opposites that never merge into a third term of synthesis. The positive term never cancels out the negative, and there is no stable equilibrium between the two but rather a constant back-and-forth, sometimes emphasizing one, sometimes the other.

The Hasidic man, as an "eternal seeker," has opted (not definitively, otherwise he would have chosen and, once and for all, be trapped in a system) for a philosophy of caress, in which there is never a rush to end things definitively. On the contrary, there is the production of the future. Here emerges a wisdom of uncertainty, of objective uncertainty. What is said about faith can be transposed into other worldly perceptions:

"Do I have faith? I cannot have any immediate certainty about this, because faith is precisely this dialectical oscillation, which, between fear and dread, never despairs. It is this infinite concern for oneself, the concern to know whether one has faith, and it is precisely this concern that is faith."

For the "seeker," for the Hasidic man, there is only one

certainty, that of the danger of the absolute.

When Rabbi Nahman says that "the world is a narrow bridge, suspended over the abyss," where man is in danger of falling at any moment from one side or the other, it means the objective uncertainty of man, in relation to the world, to the Other, and to himself. In fact, it is the movement of uncertainty that is our sign of relation with the Other; this uncertainty is the characteristic sign of "belief."

It is precisely when the individual is unsure of his relationship with the Other that he can establish a relationship with him. In the domain of faith, "when man is unsure of his relationship with God, that is exactly when he maintains it. Unfortunately, those who believe they are in a relationship with God are certainly not."

CHAPTER V

Reading, Opening, Freedom

Hasidism emphasizes a fundamental idea, already expressed and invented by the Talmudic masters, but one that has been forgotten: the Jewish people are not the "people of the book," but the "people of the interpretation of the book."

Reading is the essential activity of the Jew, through which he refuses all semantic determinisms that would predispose him to a certain determination of being. Reading is a philosophical and also political act. Reading is not a referendum in which the reader has no choice but to choose between a yes and a no, between acceptance and rejection. Reading is a political act, as the freedom of interpretation is also a freedom that marks existence. Continuing what we call "the manifesto of Rabbi Nahman of Breslov," we must quote this beautiful text by Serge Viderman:

"The text becomes the place of a singular and privileged experience, a recreation where each reader can become the center, and, even if for a short time, can escape from this passivity in which they impoverish themselves and by which they are isolated from the text whose meaning always and necessarily escapes them in large part, since being fixed by the author and belonging solely to him, the reader takes no part in it.

Let the reader learn that they are not the amazed or bored spectator of a finished story in which they have no part. Let them know only that the text speaks to them and to their own history, and soon the plurality of possible meanings will appear. The reader will learn that the text brings to them, in a coded language that does not belong to them and that they must decode, the nocturnal breath of their distant, hidden, and unspeakable life.

This means that there is no fixed meaning of the text, that the truth of the text is everywhere and nowhere, that everyone has the power to make meanings exist, to decide meanings…" The truth of a reading is not the truth of the text, just as the truth of a proposition of the world is not the truth of the world. There is no true meaning of the text revealed by interpretation, but there is a true interpretation of a text. And the truth is not the adequacy to some pre-existing meanings, but it resides in the openness to such… When reading untangles, loosens, and opens to another perspective of the world, then "to interpret a text is not to give it a meaning, even a reasonable one, but to try to appreciate what variety it is made of, what dynamic it carries, and then there is truth!" In contrast, the lie is of the order of the "knot."

The Hebrew offers this reflection in the identity of the letters that form the word chéquer (shin qof resh), "lie," and the word quécher (qof shin resh), "knot." The "lie" is of the order of closing and of a repetitive, worn-out time; it is also the "mis-spoken," which slipping into the "bad to say," produces the pathological aspect of a situation. In contrast, "truth" is the opening of speech, breath, the breath opening to tomorrow.

Thus, in the absence of finding a word that adequately expresses what commentary or interpretation should be, we propose the word "opening." Why "opening"? The word does not have here the Hebrew meaning of Petiha that would be its translation. In Hebrew, Petiha means "introduction" in a historical context or a general summary of the work.

"Opening" is understood here in the sense of the expression from the Midrash and the Zohar, Patah véamar — "he opens and says" — which is on the margin of the Saying. "He opens and says," he broke the verse and said. Breaking, then, is the opening of the word, of the téva (word) that is also a box, a volume.

By exploding a literary space: the text will no longer be approached in its linearity but in its spatiality, its volume. Perhaps it should be said that the explosion of a text is what

81

will allow the passage from the text-line to the text-volume. All the elements of the text will be subject to this explosion, this opening: the letters, the words, the sentences, the books... To illustrate what we understand by "opening," we wish to cite a beautiful page from Jankélévitch's book Somewhere in the Unfinished. A work that specifically deals with "opening." In the page we transcribe below, there are no precise rules of Hasidic hermeneutics but, it is intuitively placed in the process of opening.

"The study consists of thinking deeply about everything that can be thought in a given question, no matter the cost. One acts to untangle the inextricable and does not stop until it becomes impossible to go further; in view of this rigorous search, the words that support the thought must be used in all possible positions, in the most varied locutions. One must combine them in all their facets, in the hope that a flash will arise, palpate them and listen to their sounds to perceive the secret of their meanings; the dissonances and resonances of words are not an inspiring virtue? This rigor must be attained, sometimes at the cost of an unreadable discourse; to the point that little remains in it that does not contradict itself; it is necessary to continue along the same line, to slip along the same slope, to distance oneself more and more from the starting point, and the starting point ends up contradicting the arrival point.

It is this flawless discourse to which I subject myself, this strenge wissenschaft, rigorous science, which is not the science of the wise, but an asceticism. I feel momentarily restless when, after having for a long time, gone in circles, dug and crushed words, explored their semantic resonances, analyzed their allusive powers and their evoking potential, I realize that I cannot decisively serve any other.

For some, the pretension of one day reaching the truth is a dogmatic utopia, what matters is to go as far as one can in what is possible, to attain a flawless coherence, to bring to the surface the most hidden issues, the most unspeakable ones, to make a flat world."

Let us not be deceived! The flat world Jankélévitch speaks of does not allow one to seize the text, to understand its meaning. For the existence of levels of meaning and the rules of interpretation make it impossible to appropriate the text, and therefore to annul its alterity and exteriority. In summary, interpretation, or interpretations, never cut the text, never bite into the flesh of the text. There lies the guarantee of its inexhaustible richness.

Signs — objects, biblical verses, people, situations, and rituals — function as perfect signs:
"Whatever modifications that may be introduced into their sensitive texture, they maintain their privilege of revealing the same meanings or new aspects of those same meanings."

Perfect signs because:
"Never does the meaning of these symbols give total freedom to the materiality of the symbols that suggest them and which always retain some unsuspected power to renew this meaning, never does the spirit give freedom to the letter that reveals it. On the contrary, the spirit awakens in the letter new possibilities for suggestion."

CHAPTER VI

The Infinite Caress of the Book
A Struggle Against Idolatry

As a set of perfect signs, the Text is never tainted; one could say it is caressed. Thus, despite the work of analysis, search, clarification, and exposure, the text hides itself, remains inaccessible, always yet to come. It presents itself briefly and then withdraws. The text is at once "visible and invisible," an ambiguity, the opening and closing of meanings, an enigma.

However, the Text only hides itself if we allow it to hide; the interruption of the demonstration of transcendence, the necessary movement of retraction, depends primarily, and essentially, on the interpreter, on their way of being in relation to the text, on their way of approaching it. This way of being, this relationship with the text, we call "caress."

"The caress consists of not clinging to anything, of seeking what continually escapes from its form towards a future (never too distant) in order to find what is hidden as if it did not yet exist."

In a word, the caress is a search. In this search, the caress does not know what it seeks. This "not knowing," this "fundamental disorder," is the essence of this way of being. The relationship with the Text, which authorizes the transcendence of its voice, is like "a game absolutely without project or plan."

Hasidic study, as a search, truly allows one to "make" an experience. At this level, one can oppose the expressions "having" an experience and "making" an experience.

"Having" refers to possession, to knowing, to settling into satisfaction, to the trust that seeks to acquire; in "having," the experience is confirmed by repetition. But, as a repeated and confirmed experience, it is not something that "becomes new." From this moment on, what was once unexpected is now anticipated. "Having" an experience of the Text is to understand it without holding onto or possessing it, for it makes sense in and through repetition; we then return to "destiny." When it becomes visible, graspable, the Text takes on the form and status of an idol. Its language becomes totalitarian: "wooden language that ends up coagulating into possessed and definitively imposed meanings, ignoring situations and experiences that could change." The Text-idol is "imposed and sometimes crushed by its own weight and inflexibility."

"Making" an experience with the Text.
In "making," studying no longer means a knowledge directed toward a desired result. Nothing must correspond to our expectations. "Making" an experience is, to begin with, an experience of negativity: the thing is not what we suppose. Our knowledge and its objective mutually modify each other with the experience of another objective.

"Making" an experience is to enter into the opening, into the opening. Thus, the "man of experience" (in our context, the interpreter) is not only one who becomes an interpreter thanks to experiences (acquired), but one who is open to experiences: to hidouch (innovation).

"The fullness of experience, the fullness of being of that which we call experienced, does not consist of what man already knows entirely and well. The man of experience stands, on the contrary, radically alien to all dogmatism."

The interpreter "makes an experience" through the caress: never clinging to anything, "he sends one meaning to another and this infinitely and negatively, so that when one wishes to locate (in the Text) a center, an origin for the meanings, a god to give it meaning, one can find in it (in the Text) only emptiness, the emptiness of language, the blank spaces of writing."

It is then understood why study finds its graphic memory in the letter Lamed, the only one of the twenty-two letters of the Hebrew alphabet to cross the line of writing, to transgress, to cast itself "beyond the verse." Lamed, the final letter of the Torah.

The Letter Lamed

A Struggle Against Idolatry

In fact, we can summarize the meaning of Hasidic study as a struggle against idolatry. The study is, at the same time, a theological and political gesture, but the theological is not where it is expected.

The Hasidic man does not say "God is," for this dogmatic assertion is also idolatrous. He does not even say "God is not." He feels, so to speak, an atheistic necessity by rejecting the text-idol. It is for this reason that the Text will remain untouchable, impregnable, and will not take on the form or place of an idol. Kabbalists explain that the Text, the Torah, and God are one (Rahamana véqoudcha bérikh hou, had hou). By refusing to imprison the Text, he simultaneously refuses to lay hands on the divine. The relationship with the text and with God is also paradoxical: one must distance oneself, such distance is necessary so that the relationship with God is not idolatrous. This is what Henri Atlan radically terms "the atheism of scripture."

"The primary concern of biblical teaching is not the existence of God, a deism in opposition to atheism, but rather the struggle against idolatry. Now, there is a danger of idolatry in any deism. All deism is idolatry because the expression gives it meaning and, therefore, coagulates it; unless, in some way, its discourse denies itself and becomes atheistic. In other words, the paradoxes of language and its meanings are such that the only discourse about God that is not idolatrous is the atheistic discourse. Or yet, the only discourse in which God is not an idol is the one in which God is not a god."

All the masters of Jewish thought, from the prophets to contemporary scholars, understood this...

The system of interpretation (besides its necessity for the phenomenon of understanding) is based on the will to refuse idolatry. The Text, the first relationship with God, must not become an idol. The idolatrous temptation is so strong that it appeals to us even the day after the Revelation, the Golden Veil: the temptation of appearance and Presence. "The idol shows us the divine, where there is neither illusion nor disillusion." The idol (and here the Text takes on the meaning of a manual) calms; the idol brings closer:

"The idol works precisely to reduce the distance and separation from the divine... When the absence of the divine occurs, the idol places it at our disposal, assures it, and ultimately deforms it. As the idol becomes complete, the divine fades away mortally. The idol tries to make us approach and appropriate the divine: this is why it fears atheism, the worshiper takes hold of the divine in the form of a god, but by imprisoning it, he loses what he had: nothing remains but a well-known, manipulable, and guaranteed amulet... The idol breaks the distance that identifies and authenticates the divine as such (as that which does not belong to us but happens to us)."

Chapter VII: Reading is a Revolution

The Hebrew language, like other Semitic languages, has a tri-consonantal root, consisting of three consonants: vowels are not part of the root (traditional Hebrew texts are generally written without vowels).

The Hebrew root, formed mostly by three spaced consonants, opens a field of extraordinary significance. It unfolds multiple readings, based on an undetermined starting point (in its non-vocalized status). Thus, Hebrew presents an unfinished nature that demands completion from the reader.

The vowels (or more precisely, the vowel points) close the indeterminacy and openness of the root and, through their introduction, produce a much more restricted sound and meaning, allowing verbal communication.

"A single root is not always composed of the same vowels, which generates a semantic core that is malleable, plastic, and flexible."

"The core of the word will vary and transform, modifying the vowel points over the same root, with the meaning changing to the point of being so different that it can become confusing as soon as it appears."

The absence of vowels is of great importance. It removes the exclusivity of one meaning, leaving the root in its initial indeterminacy, susceptible to being differently informed.

Thus, we are responsible for words.

A verse from the Book of Numbers states that the children of Israel departed from the mountain of God on a journey of three days. The Midrash offers the following interpretation:

"What does it mean, 'They departed from the Mountain of God on a three-day journey'? This means that the children of

Israel sought the mountain of Sinai as a child who fled from school after learning much."

Rabbi Yossef Rozin explains the text like this:

"As a child who fled from school means: they did not want to learn the letters of the Torah as separate entities, but preferred to read and study whole words."

These comments question a relationship with the text that sees it as a finished totality, an object to be possessed and assimilated, like a craftsman who, in his relationship with the hand, cancels the transcendence and ecstasy of time, enclosing it in "hand-keeping." This attitude is considered by the Talmud as an extremely grave "fault," suggesting that the "reading in pieces" is a remedy for this negative attitude. Thus, we must understand why, for the Hasidic tradition, each letter is a world, each word an entire universe.

Reading letter by letter is about feeling the constitution of things, understanding the space that exists between each letter. This stratified reading spatializes the text, opening it in volume, meaning the liberation of its weight and typographic petrification.

Hasidic reading represents, in fact, a poetic experience that seeks to capture the babbling of language and the world it creates, to try to break forth into the light. This experience is very similar to that described by Bachelard when he said:

"I often imagine words as little houses, with a cellar and an attic. The common meaning resides on the ground floor, always exposed to the 'outside commerce' of someone passing through, who is never a dreamer. To climb the stairs in the house of a word is, step by step, to abstract oneself. To descend into the cellar is to dream, to lose oneself in the distant corridors of uncertain etymology, to seek treasures not yet found. To go up and down, within the words themselves, such is the life of the poet. Going very high, going very low is permitted to the poet who unites the earthly with the airy. Shall only the philosopher be condemned by his peers to live on the ground floor?"

The reader who wishes to maintain the words in the exactness of their meanings, taking them as thousands of small tools for clear thinking, would be astonished by the audacity of a Hasidic reader. And thus, the words would never crystallize into perfect solids; this is why, in everyday language, "the central meaning of the noun is surrounded by unexpected adjectives. A new ambiance allows the word to enter not only into thoughts but also into dreams. Language dreams."

What Bachelard said about the phrase producing a new ambiance is true at the level of the word itself, within the framework of Midrashic and Talmudic thought. The word is – when read letter by letter – a phrase, an infinity of phrases.

Reading is not the aggregation of a world into a word, but its fragmentation. Hasidic reading, unlike the Greek logos, does not seek to gather, enclose, and preserve. As Rabbi Yossef Rozin said, we must distinguish between the "reading of words" and the "reading of letters"; it is necessary to allow the letters to be letters, despite the existence of words.

Hasidic reading is not limited to a linguistic operation that attempts to reduce saying to a "will to say," guiding it to the shadow of a meaning, breaking the utopia of language and leading it to the topic of discourse.

Hasidic reading is an operation of dissemination that restores life, movement, and time to the heart of the word itself. It is thus that it constitutes them as works of art and distances them from the dangers of being seen as idols. Here, words are no longer finalized by meanings, but by senses. The reading breaks the instance of meaning, and all elements of the text— words, syllables, consonants, and vowels—ask and answer each other.

Reading is revolution; the life restored to language in this "fragmenting" reading is revolution. "Revolution is everywhere where a change is established that breaks the purpose of established models."

Thus, reading embodies an attitude of contestation in relation to tradition. It opposes the transmission of the stereotypes of ideological discourses. The reading of letters is an "education" in the primitive sense of the word, meaning "to lead beyond the already traced path toward progress."

Reading the letters and not the words.

The reading of words imposes a totality that obscures the difficult path of articulating one letter to another. Reading the letters, one by one, is to dream of an "other way of being," which will then have much more difficulty being inverted into a simple "being of another way." Reading the letters signifies the demand for the simultaneity of saying and unsaying, which allows the world not to be enclosed in the conditions of its enunciation.

CHAPTER VIII
Art and Language

Let us continue our journey with Rabbi Nahman of Breslov, one of the most precise masters in making us discover the Hasidic landscape.

Existential reading can be articulated with an aesthetic dimension, with a certain vision and understanding of art. Rabbi Nahman of Breslov constantly insists on this need for recreation; he would not have listened to a text without first having constructed it. To support this intuition, he cites a verse from Psalms, whose surprising formulation leads to an equally surprising interpretation.

It is written: "ossé devaro lichmoa beqol devaro"94, which certain translations have rendered as "those who fulfill their word, to be attentive to the sound of their word."

A more literal translation offers a fairer sense95: "Fabricators of His word, to understand the voice of His word."

Rabbi Nahman comments:

"Because the righteous are 'heroes of strength,' that is, they make and build the word of God, or rather, the 'holy tongue' by which the world was created...

For the righteous belong to the order of the 'fabricators of His word,' that is, they fabricate the word by which God speaks and creates the world.

All of this took place before the creation of the world. But even now, when the righteous wish to hear a word from God, they first make it, build it, and fabricate it. That is to say: through their positive actions, they achieve the ability to hear divine words.

It is necessary to understand that these words come from and have been constructed by their hands.

This corresponds to the verse from Psalms: 'Fabricators of His words to hear His word,' for as soon as they wish to understand the word, they make it: 'doers of words.' It is only afterward that they understand this word, as it is written: 'to understand the voice of His word,' for it is in this word that God speaks to them."

This absolutely fundamental text raises a "logic of listening" that is deeply revolutionary.

Man cannot understand something in the text unless he constructs (boné), fabricates, and makes (ossé) this word. Refusing the passivity of language, man does not settle into an already constituted, pre-made language; he must first model it, whether through his own language, his own word, or the word of God. This is not the inversion of the transcendence of the divine word into its radical immanence; it is, on the contrary, an essential modality of the possibility of a transcendent word. The fact that Rabbi Nahman speaks of "hands," of "actions" to describe the word, reinforces the active side of this word. He generalizes in his own way the "saying is doing" and, in doing so, explains a "theorem-phrase" of Jewish thought:
Naassé Venichma, whose explanation is often given as: "Let us do and we will understand." Let us act first and react afterward. It is necessary to revisit this statement to understand it:
"Let us first make the words that will allow us to understand them," let us do so as to enter into the activity of language. A language that constructs a world, and not the world.
The terms constructed by the "fabricators of words" are not tools or instruments by which the world will be impacted; the constructed words are "works of art." The term "work of art" is characterized by an "irreducibility" in the world.

At this point, it is necessary to clarify the distinction between the instrument and the work of art, to bring out the difference between an instrumental reading and an artistic reading.

The fact that a functioning instrument does not draw attention to itself is an indication that it is entirely reduced to its use, in the context to which it belongs.

The work of art is, on the contrary, precisely characterized, placed in the most common aesthetic experience, by the fact that it imposes itself as worthy of attention in and of itself. It does not limit itself to the world to which it belongs; it stands out from it, and even if it addresses the real, as in the case of contemporary works (e.g., Duchamp), it surpasses the work by this detachment that is generally constituted by a system of framing and limitation that reinforces the distance.

Moreover, this distancing, this detachment, is not meant to underline the provenance of any given world, but, on the contrary, to point to another world, a new world.

The work, in itself, carries its own world. A world to come that it grounds and institutes.

Thus, it does not need to be situated historically in a contextual world. The work of art neither expresses nor witnesses a constituted world: it itself realizes and grounds it. The work of art is a radical novelty. In our terminology, it is a hidouch. Just like the hidouch, it opens a general perspective on the world, which engages in dialogue with our perspective and forces us to modify it, or at least deepen it.

Rabbi Nahman emphasizes the need for this transition from the "word – instrument" to the "word – work of art": invention of new meanings that do not revert to already existing meanings; the search for another word, for a life project that is openness.

Rabbi Nahman speaks of the "creation of the world"; he is not only referring to the action of creation in the cosmological and cosmogonic sense, but to the world in which man is inserted and through which he unfolds a space for project. (One might then question what the citation from the Midrash means, which states that before the "real" creation, God consulted the word of the righteous, who had not yet existed. As if the condition for creation rested upon this creative and inventive capacity brought by the righteous, of the generations to come.)

The hidouch is the word that opens and clarifies a world, proposing a new way of ordering it. The opening proposed is nothing more than a possibility of opening: that is why it speaks of a world and not the world.

The "opening word" contains a multitude of meanings. It is

the place of the "visible and invisible"97. Thus, it remains to clarify the meaning of "truth" which we define as "opening to."

In the "hidouch word," the "work of art word," creator of worlds, truth stands for the work, not only as an opening and development, but also as obscurity and dissimulation. The "opening word" thus becomes the "opening – dissimulating word," light and secret.

Once created, this word draws attention to itself, not only because it opens a world by offering a new explicit perspective but because it always presents itself as a supplementary reserve of meanings still to be discovered. This idea of a "world" that at the same time offers and dissimulates is seen in the Talmud98 in the following way: the "world" is said in Hebrew as olam (ayin-lamed-mèm); it can be vocalized in such a way that it can be read as elèm, meaning "hidden"... Thus, léolam becomes léélem: instead of "for the world," it is "to hide."

The "world" is what shows itself before us, with violence and shamelessness, exposing itself clearly to the eye! It is what belongs to the possibility of being apprehended by the eye, by thought, or by hand; it is what is given as a gift, in a "now," which I can make mine through an act of total appropriation. This pledge on the world is of the order of the always-present, of "maintaining" (a term here used in the sense of "holding in hands"). The "world" is thus excluded from the future. Even though things appear, their appearance is due to a development, the unfolding of a meaning always anticipated. To have a "world" in the sense of olam is to escape the uncertainty of the future.

The Hasidic reading produces distancing, the explosion – perhaps for the first time, one can understand here the double meaning of the word explosion, which means both rupture and brightness.

The "explosion" would be the place of this light that both withdraws and shines at the same time. "Reading in pieces," a term that denotes this Hasidic reading, is positioning oneself in a léélem, in a "for disappearing," where the path that inevitably leads to… is erased, in order to situate oneself in a furrow where memory is lost and all that had been traced before fades.

The léélem where the "world" (olam) disappears no longer allows mastery or comprehension in "maintaining." Here is what we call the philosophy of caress…

The duality of laws, that of the "written law" and the "oral law," is olam and élém, development and retraction. The retraction of the oral law collects a reserve of new meanings that are not predictable, but that the creative reading will invent.

The "constructed word," which Rabbi Nahman speaks of in relation to Psalm 103, does not only arise in the opening of the world, but it opens and institutes the very opening; it not only produces a change within the world, but modifies the very opening to the world, by force of a hidouch.

Man, upon reading, invents himself in the exact measure of his reading and thus constitutes himself a narrative identity.

Existential reading.

CHAPTER IX:
The Mahloquèt
For a Plural Word

Let us visit a "house of study"! Disorder, noise, vehement gesticulation, constant comings and goings—this is how the Beth Hamidrach presents itself: the house of study that takes place in the synagogue, and often in the dining room as well. Hasidic students do not have the serenity of monks. Silence is not the rule; on the tables, rarely aligned, there is confusion, with books from the Torah, Maimonides, and the Shulchan Aruch; books are open, piled one on top of another.

The students—sitting, standing, one knee on the bench or chair—are leaning over the texts; from one corner to another, but more frequently facing one another, they read aloud, swaying back and forth, from left to right, punctuating difficult-to-understand passages with long thumb gestures, frantically tapping the books or tables, sometimes even the shoulder of their study companion, feverishly flipping through the pages of the commentaries, which are quickly taken and returned to the shelves of the immense library surrounding the room. The protagonists of this "war of meaning" seek to understand, interpret, and explain.

Rarely agreeing on the meaning of the studied passage, they consult the master, who explains, takes a position on the proposed theses, and momentarily calms the passionate debate of the inquirers. On another, more distant table, one student sleeps, arms crossed over a Talmudic text, while another drinks coffee and smokes a cigarette, adopting a meditative air, the necessary concentration to continue the study. A great mess! The Beth Hamidrach knows an uninterrupted effervescence, where day or night, the voices resound, the infinite murmur of study.

We offer this description of the house of study because it seems revealing of the Talmudic and Hasidic way of thinking. Perhaps here we can best feel the dimension and political function of the Talmudic and Hasidic worlds, that is, their anti-ideological aspect.

The Hasidic revolution, as already shown, consists of escaping from a dogmatic and institutionalized word. The Hasidic word opens life through life, making things and beings dance. The first dimension of an anti-ideological and anti-dogmatic word is the situation of dialogue.

The dialogue, or more precisely, the situation of dialogue, does not mean agreement. Perhaps it can be understood as an "accord" in the musical sense of the term, the plurality of notes that produces a richer sound. The difference of opinion is a sign of social health.

The ethics of Hasidism, as found, for example, in the texts of Rabbi Nahman of Breslav, is essentially the uninterrupted significance of meaning, and in doing so, Hasidism restores to each individual the possibility of producing their own opinion.

To have an opinion does not mean adhering to a dogmatic belief blindly; the opinion becomes a pure reflection of the diversity of aspects of the world.

Contrary to the concept, the dogma, and the truth that presuppose the unity, the One of reality, the opinion has the characteristic of being able to oppose other opinions, sometimes diametrically opposite, which together reflect various aspects of an ontologically plural reality.

The plural word has a name: in the Talmud, it is called Mahloquèt.

The reversals and historical deviations of messianic or pseudo-messianic currents, the need to establish a general law for enabling collective life, produced a distrust of opinion and free thought. The brilliance of the Talmudic and Midrashic word in its dialogical conception was completely forgotten, in fact, hidden.

Hasidic thinking, in its essence, seeks to renew, to reconnect with this fundamental aspect of the Talmudic text and spirit.

Mahloquèt means that it is impossible to find unity solely through texts. The Hasidic individual always seeks a study companion to "counter" him or her.

We will proceed here in two stages. After an exposition of Mahloquèt as it can be found in the Talmud, we will show the more Hasidic formulation given to it by Rabbi Nahman of Breslav, who insisted on the word as questioning.

In a quickly sketched typology, one can oppose a "one-dimensional" world to a "two-dimensional" world.

The Talmudic world is two-dimensional, and in this, it is markedly anti-ideological. The Talmudist—the "true" one—never says: "We"; he no longer has the right to say: "The Talmud says..." He can say: "There is an opinion in the Talmud that states... but there is also an opinion that says exactly the opposite..."

The first thing that jumps to the eye of the Talmud reader is the importance of dialogue in the sequential formulation of thought. Rarely are there elements without controversy, to the point that as soon as one speaks of "a notion," one says: Mahloquèt ploni véploni, that is: "discussion between so-and-so (master)." Talmudic thought is often formulated in a polemical manner: discussion between Hillel and Shammai, Rav and Shmuel, Rav Huna and Rav Hisda, Abaye and Rava, Rabbi Yohanan and Reish Lakish, etc.

In Mahloquèt, reconciliation is not sought. If one wants to use a term from dialectics—often employed for the Talmudic method—it must be said to be an "open dialectic," for no synthesis, no third term, will suppress the contradiction. The "Whole" does not reconcile itself in the "Same," in the identity

100

of the identical and the non-identical. Mahloquèt is a way of saying and thinking the refusal of synthesis and system: anti-dogmatism that allows only a living truth.

Regarding the Talmudic discussions, the Talmud says: "The words of one and the other are the words of the living God."

It is necessary to understand this phrase conditionally: "If there are words of one and the other, then they are the words of the living God, and therefore, they are alive." The goal of Mahloquèt is to undo satisfaction, undo "knowing where thought always shows itself in its scale."

Mahloquèt leads us on the path of a non-conceptual thought, "diversity gathers in the presence of representation; accepting synchronicity, it confirms its ability to enter into the unity of a genre or form: everything can be thought together: Thought of the Presence."

The thought of the kind "Everything is present here and now."

Mahloquèt shows precisely that nothing can be reduced to the "Same," nothing can be bound to synchronicity and synthesis; it also shows that perception is not simply "understanding" or "seizing."

Mahloquèt is the only possibility for the event of thought to develop into thinking thought.

Mahloquèt: the battle against "thought thought," or against the death of thought and, as "Maharal" of Prague says, against death.

In fact, in the word Mahloquèt, one can read M-hlq-t, which means that duality refuses the term "death" (mèt) the possibility of constituting itself. The logical structure of Mahloquèt is that of the "book." Write and erase (stroke), say and unsay.

As soon as a master proposes a thought, his interlocutor shakes it from its position, from its positivity: incessant destabilization, atheistic thinking that resists synchronization, thus leading to a stage in infinity.

An Open Dialectic

To define Mahloquèt, it is necessary first to define the expression "open dialectic," which means that the spirit opens itself to the recognition of the opposition of another spirit: transcendence of the self as the acceptance of leaving the world, the constitution of the "Other" before me. Here are three reference points that help clarify this notion of "open dialectic":

First, study and thought are only possible through an experience of dialogue.

Secondly, dialogue is not simply an exchange of ideas, but "questions and answers" (chéélot ou téchouvot).

Finally, the question and the answer do not evolve within the same sphere of thought.

Thus, two types of dialogue experience, two types of dialectic, can be opposed. The Talmudic and Hasidic Mahloquèt would be a "transcendent dialectic," because the Other-person in the dialogue is not a figure of style; the interlocutor does not play the role of testing the speaker. To better understand what Talmudic dialogue is, one can oppose it to what it is not: here we can evoke Plato and the so-called "Platonic" dialogues.

"The reference to Plato is only enlightening negatively. It helps us discard all the false aspects of dialogue. The Socratic dialogue is not a true dialogue, because it is entirely based on the postulate of the unity of Reason as the place of truth, even if this place is somewhat still to be discovered, nevertheless, it is always there."

For Plato, Truth as Truth is "One" and is attained through reminiscence. The dialogue becomes, therefore, an artifice of the logos, and the duality of characters and voices that are heard are merely a path toward the One. The dialogue is purely dialectical, an ornamented and eminently skillful form

103

of discourse.

In this sense, Platonic dialectic is an "immanent dialectic." The interlocutor, in most cases, contentedly says: "Yes...!", "No...", "Exactly...", "I think that too...", etc. In reality, it is the central character of the dialogue who formulates the questions and answers.

"Everything takes place within the same consciousness; an interior discourse where thought artificially divides itself in order to question and answer itself, until everything is renewed."

In "immanent dialectic," thought remains the same:

"It moves from one term to its opposite, which evokes it, but the dialectic in which it finds itself is not a dialogue, or it is the dialogue of the soul with itself, arising through questions and answers, an interior discourse where the spirit, while thinking, does not become less one and unique, despite its steps and the back-and-forth through which it can oppose itself."

The Talmudic master, and the Hasidic thinker, at a certain point in their search, know that they know; their study in dialogue does not aim, therefore, for the comfort of a pre-existing knowledge. On the contrary, they seek to be shaken, disturbed, put to the test, and laid bare.

Learning is not about acquiring knowledge that has existed since eternity in the empyrean; learning is not "reminiscence," and teaching is not "maieutics."

Chapter X: The Energy of Questioning

The Mahloquèt as the foundation of Talmudic and Hasidic thought is essentially tied to a particular conception of hermeneutics and truth. The fact that the same text can offer numerous interpretations indicates that there is no "exact" interpretation. This leads us to move away from the binary logic of true and false (Greek logic) and enter into what we call the "logic of meaning."

As Nietzsche rightly said: "There are many kinds of eyes... and consequently, there are many kinds of truth, and therefore, no truth at all."

To truly enter Hasidic thought, every time a certainty is affirmed, one must seek the opposite affirmation with which this certainty is related. Hasidic thought, therefore, never ceases to oppose itself, never content with itself, never satisfied with this opposition.

This mode of thought corresponds to a word whose modality maintains the dynamic demand. It is the action, in our eyes, of the "questioning word," the question.

"The question is movement... In the simple grammatical structure of the interrogation, we already perceive this openness of the questioning word; in it is the need for something else; incomplete, the word that questions affirms that it is only a part. The question is, therefore, essentially partial; it is the place where the word is always found in an unfinished way..."

The question, as an unfinished word, takes support in the incomplete. It is not incomplete as a question; on the contrary, by declaring itself incomplete, it is complete. Through the question, we "give ourselves to the thing" and provide the emptiness that allows us not to have it yet or to have it only as the desire of thought.

Hasidic thought is a thinking of inquiry, and it is no accident that the first word of the Talmud is precisely a question: Méématai ("From when?").

Rabbi Nahman of Breslav explains that the inter-relational space of Mahloquèt proceeds from hallal hapanouï, the empty space necessary for creation. God withdraws: He leaves an "empty space" (hallal hapanouï) that is essentially the place of origin for all questions, as it contains within itself the question of questions: the Enigma! Indeed, God withdraws, so He is absent! But can there be anything outside of the vitality infused by the divine? No! Therefore, God is present. Yéchvé-ayïn ("Being and nothing") coexist at the same time. When two masters discuss together, the relationship proceeds from this paradox; this is called Bina. This word does not designate a quality or intellectual capacity but a rational attitude of dialogue that must be maintained.

What exists between two opposing masters?

"Nothing more essential than the Nothing itself (the emptiness in the middle, an interval that always deepens and, as it deepens, fills itself). Nothing as work and movement."

A text from Pirqué Avot (a classic text of Talmudic literature) says: "All my life, I have grown among the masters." According to Rabbi Nahman, this maxim means: "I have grown 'between' (beyne), that is, in the space of nothing, in the emptiness that separates and unites the masters in a situation of Mahloquèt."

To maintain the paradoxical relationship in action in Mahloquèt, the question should not await an answer: "The answer is the misfortune of the question." Indeed, through the question, things are brought, transformed into "possibilities," dramatically elevated to their possibility, beyond their being. Answering would bring back to being what was beyond. The answer suppresses the "openness," the richness of possibility; now, the role of the question is precisely to open. The question "inaugurates a type of relationship characterized by openness and free movement."

In the context of an interpretive problem, the question assumes a privileged place and here takes on the meaning of "putting into question." Hermeneutics, that is, the art of interpreting, and not the art of repeating, implies the suspension of our own prejudices. Every suspension of judgment, especially that of prejudices, has from a logical point of view the structure of a question. The essence of the question is of the order of opening and leaving the possibilities open...

The opening of what is asked resides in the unfixity of the answer. The required thing must remain in suspension... placed in such a way that the "against" balances the "for." A question does not find its meaning unless it undergoes this suspension that makes it an open question.

"Every authentic question requires this openness."

The Tradition of the New!

The thinking of the thinker begins with admiration. He does not aim to be "admired," but rather to "admire himself." Hasidic admiration is not a reaction to the world; it is a deliberate, voluntary, totally active, and creative act. The origin of this admiration is not found in the world, but in man.

Admiration should primarily be based on what surrounds us: time, space, things, like-minded people, animals, plants, tools, etc., and ourselves.
Paradoxically, the question does not aim at the Unknown, the mysterious and invisible worlds, distant and difficult to access; it does not aim at "past worlds," but at the "near" and the "immediate," everything that is close and encountered "at every moment."
Why?
"Because what we encounter 'at every moment' is not the near, but the habitual. [Now] the habitual carries within it this terrible power of unaccustoming us to dwell in the essential and, most often, in such a decisive way that it no longer allows us to reach that place to dwell in."

Every personal existence is a reprise of a pre-personal tradition. However, the meaning of this tradition (despite its effective transmission) gets lost and is often forgotten: "Man in the world always moves upon the ground of an unanalyzed tradition, and for a long time, impenetrable."
Man is essentially a "traditional being," meaning:
"He succumbs to a tradition, whether he knows it or not, more or less explicitly. This tradition frees him from the duty of guiding his own life, of raising a radical question, and of making a decisive choice... The tradition, which thus imposes its supremacy, far from making accessible what it 'transmits,' contributes, on the contrary, most of the time, to hiding it. It degrades its evident content and blocks access to the original 'sources,' where the categories and traditional concepts were, at least in part, truly thought. It suppresses any need to understand why one should return to the sources."

It is here that the question, the admiration, intervenes ("insofar as, on this occasion, man witnesses the ruin of the traditions of his knowledge, his pre-understandings of the world and the facts), and he feels the need for a new explanation of the world." To revive a decayed and hardened tradition, to eliminate the burdens it has accumulated over time, to free itself from the debris it has deposited, one must adopt a fundamentally critical attitude, which can be called destruction to highlight its radicality and importance. It is a positive act of destruction that should allow man "to open himself to the new and, so to speak, to open himself originally to the world, to enter into the dawn of a new day in the world, where he himself and everything else begin to emerge under a new light, where the world offers itself to him in a new way." This idea of the novelty of perception, in understanding the world and things, is a constant in Talmudic thought, Midrashic thought, and even more evidently in Hasidic thought, among masters like the author of Sefat Hemet, Rabbi Nahman of Breslov, or Rabbi Tsadoq Hakohen of Lublin!

It is the notion of Hitadechout that serves as the main reference in the commentaries on verse 16 of chapter 26 of Deuteronomy: "Hayom hazé hachem Eloquékha metsavékha laassot: 'Today God commands you to do...'"

The Midrash Tanhuma asks:

"What does 'today' mean? (Hayom hazé). Hadn't the Holy One—blessed be He—commanded anything until now? Therefore, the 'today' in question is situated in the fortieth year after the Revelation. Here is what must be understood: 'Moses said to Israel: The Torah should be so dear to you that every day should be to you as if it were the very day of the Revelation (as if on this day you received it from Mount Sinai).'"

We have another version of this Midrash, given by Rashi in his commentary on the cited verse. It is in light of this version that it is generally repeated by commentators:

"Today means that they (the commandments) should be considered before your eyes as if they were new (Yiyou beénékha kéhadachim)."

The continuation of this Midrash, rarely cited, is of crucial importance:

"Rabbi Yohanan says: One who performs the Torah (Kol haossé èt Hatora) according to its truth (laamitah) is considered as having made himself (as if he had made himself), as it says: At that time (baèt hahi) God commanded me to teach you these rules and laws so that 'you may do them' (laassotekhèm otam...). It does not say 'you may do them' (laassot otam), but 'you make yourselves' (laassotekhem atèm); thus, man creates himself, makes himself (hou assa ouvara èt atsmo)."

From this Midrash, we can make some observations about the motives and goals of the "questioning attitude." Admiration and questioning "make man depart from the fundamental world of his routine life, out of the negligence and metaphysical laziness in which he has ceased to question the world..."

The admiration and questioning (Hokhma) lead man out of the obligation of daily familiarity with the world (pre-established, traditional, and archaic familiarity), into the creative indigence of not knowing.

Through admiration and questioning, man will be able to liberate himself, once and for all, from the prison (even unconscious) of certain thinking habits, convictions, unverified theories, opinions, prejudices, and ready-made decisions that decree what the world, things, people, knowledge, etc., are.

Up to this point, the function of Hokhma has been presented on a theoretical level, so to speak, within the framework of a "theory of knowledge." The Midrash we cited, in turn, seems to insist on knowledge of being and doing, as well as on the relationship between being and knowing.

Kol yom kéhadachim, which could be translated as "tradition of the new," requires, after the moment of "positive destruction," a reactivation of meaning...

Hidouch, the "innovation of meaning," always strives to go beyond pre-established meaning. One does not leave the habitual to find the origin; the movement is not regressive. On the contrary, there is an imperative will to construct meaning to build the development of History. The reactivation awakens

110

the creative power of interpretation. It is not the meaning that is reactivated, but rather the power of the word, the event, or the act of meaning both and beyond.

THIRD PART
BODY AND WRITING

A Small Treatise on Hebrew Meditation

It is forbidden to be old.
Rabbi Nahman of Breslov

Introduction

After having addressed the major historical and philosophical
outlines of Hasidism, we will propose in this third part a
fundamental aspect, yet little known, of Jewish mysticism,
devoted to meditation and certain bodily practices that lead
to the discovery of the inner universe and experiences of
elevation and privileged relationships with the divine.
This aspect of Judaism has been extremely hidden and
repelled, to the point that it appears, even to the eyes of
specialists, as delirium or heresy. However, there exists a
meditative mysticism whose most important precursor was
Rabbi Abraham Abulafia (1240 – 1292). In this field, one also
speaks of ecstatic Kabbalah or prophetic Kabbalah. Hasidic
mysticism, as found among the early masters and particularly
with Baal Shem Tov, directly belongs to this lineage of Ecstatic
Kabbalah.

Hebrew meditation comprises several aspects:

Combinatory recitations of words and names
Breathing techniques
Dynamic visualization of Hebrew letters
Body movements and postures

CHAPTER I
Meditation and Health

The goal of meditation is to elevate oneself and seek better physical, spiritual, and intellectual balance: the pleasure of being. Well-being in the world.
Even though, for certain masters like Abulafia, the goal of meditation was ecstasy or what is called the prophetic experience, another formulation of this goal can be used, that of the health of being. Understanding the exact meaning of the term health expressed in Hebrew will help to better grasp the objectives and functioning of meditation.

In Hebrew, health is referred to as Beriyout (Bèt-rèch-yod-aleph-vav-tav). The adjective healthy is bari (bèt-rèch-yod-aleph) in the masculine and beria (bèt-rèch-yod-aleph-hé) in the feminine.

It is very important to note that these words come from the same root as Beriya, which means "creation of the world," and the verb bara, meaning "to create."
To be in good health, then, for Hebrew thought, is to be in a position of "creation," in the incessant recreation of oneself and the world.
Beriyout establishes itself in a dynamically conscious body and mind.
This dynamism is possible when a person does not see themselves as a finished structure but as the place of the birth of themselves and, consequently, the world.
We will see later that Beriya is the passage from nothingness to being, represented in its infinitesimal manifestation by the point that will then undergo the metamorphoses of "formation."
Health, viewed as creation, necessitates a return to the situation of the emergence of being. It is necessary to not see the world as it is, but in its "way" of being, its "way" of being born.
And, since the relationship between man and the world essentially passes through a linguistic translation, a language

in the process of unfolding is necessary to order this creation. From this, it is understood why there is a set of techniques to put language in motion, allowing for a new word to be born in each combination.

To be in good health (Beriya) is to be a creature (Beriya) that perceives and lives as if it were in the process of being born. It is in this perspective that Kabbalah addresses the dialectic of Ani and Ayin, the "I" and the "Nothing."
In Hebrew, the word "I" is Ani, written aleph-noun-yod; three letters that also spell Ayin, aleph-yod-noun, meaning "nothing."
This provisional "nothinging" (nadização) is the key to the dynamism of being (see Chapter IV).
The goal of meditation is to maintain the dynamism of being, which in Hebrew is called ratsone and means "will" to us.
Ratsone is more than mere will. It is the desire to live, a deep vital impulse, characterized by a creative internal tension, announcing itself as the pulse of life, establishing the person as a being in the making.

Beriyout-health consists of allowing the expression of ratsone, a renewed experience of creative energy that allows man to tend toward a "further" in order to elevate themselves to a "higher."
This inner energy of constantly reinventing oneself, which man possesses, is called Simha, meaning "joy," whose Hebrew letters also spell the word Messiah.
Indeed, the word hasimha (joy) can be rewritten as machiah, which means "Messiah."
To bear the "Messiah" is to feel this movement of being vibrate within oneself, which is to desire and want to be

CHAPTER II
Joy as Therapy

Hasidism is a defense in favor of a joyful and happy existence. With Baal Shem Tov, sadness disappeared.
We have outlined the major lines of Hasidic thought, which present themselves as an ethic of renewal in thought and action. In a phrase by Rabbi Nahman of Breslov, we understand the essence of these lines of thought: "It is forbidden to be old."

The ethic of renewal is based on defining man as a being of desire (ratsone). This capacity to be different tends toward joy and is joy itself: Simha.

Joy is sometimes both the goal and the very place of desire; it is that inner force man possesses, which drives him toward the future.
"Existence is not merely an indefinite journey, a perpetual differentiation; it is also oriented toward a goal called the joy of existing."

But attention! It is never total fullness, for here, once again, we must underline that the perfection of man is his perfectibility (Neher).
The Hasidic openness is an adventure of joy.
Rabbi Nahman of Breslov formulated this categorical imperative: Mitsva guedola liyehot besimha tamid: "It is a great mitzvah (commandment) to always be in joy."
"Sadness is the exile of the divine presence," he also said. But when a person performs an act in joy, he opens himself to the future miracle, releasing the sparks of holiness imprisoned in beings.
The joy of action liberates the sparks, but the liberation of the sparks is the source of joy itself.
When joy takes over a person's body, their hands and feet rise. They can no longer stop themselves from dancing.

Some unforgettable aphorisms by Rabbi Nahman, found in his

work Liquté Moharan, clearly show the relationship between joy and creation or liberation... "Joy is what allows a person to innovate with new meanings in the Torah."
In chapter 24 of Liquté, Rabbi Nahman develops a very important dialectic where he shows the impossibility of reaching infinity through desire and joy. There is always an antagonistic force that pulls in the opposite direction. The dynamics of the search are conditioned by a radical impossibility of reaching infinity. Without this, a person would cancel themselves out definitively.

Joy holds such an important place in Hasidism that it even conditions illness and healing. For Rabbi Nahman, for example, all diseases have only one origin: sadness.
"It is a great mitzvah to always be in joy, to defend oneself and distance oneself from sadness and bitterness with all one's might.
All diseases that come upon a person arise from the degradation of joy... The degradation of joy comes from a distortion of the 'deep song' (nigoun), of the ten vital rhythms (Defiquim)."

When joy and song (nigoun) are shaken, illness takes hold of the person. Joy is a great remedy. It is the ability to find within oneself a single positive point that makes us light and fixes the joy.
Joy is the creation of a space where words can give themselves, exist.
Just as laughter, in its clamor, alters the sound space, amplifies it, and opens its field of resonance, joy is also linked to the ability to express oneself, that is, to break the chains of introspection, of the circle of ready-made words and thoughts. Joy is this ability that a person has to reinvent themselves.

Joy is a dance, a circle game that finds the strength to open a link and breathe new life into existence.

CHAPTER III
Meditation and Pleasure

In the Kabbalistic tradition originating from the school of Abraham Abulafia, the goal of meditation is to reach levels of knowledge similar to those of prophetic experience. Prophetic experience is achieved through a set of techniques involving the recitation of divine Names and key words, combined with techniques of breathing and visualization. For Abulafia, this prophetic experience should lead a person to unite with the celestial powers and open the paths to the immortality of the soul.

It is important to note: unlike many mystical doctrines that recommended asceticism to reach ecstatic states, Abulafia believed that no ascetic behavior was necessary for one who aimed to attain prophecy. In Hebrew meditation, there is no devaluation of matter and the body as found in Neoplatonic literature. There is no struggle between intellect and body, or intellect and soul.

Abulafia takes an audacious direction, using certain erotic and sexual images, which are not only metaphors to demonstrate the mystical relationship between man and the powers above, but which reinforce the idea that pleasure is united with prophetic experience. "One could say, as Moshe Idel mentions, that what is happening here is merely a theoretical analogy between the image of the sexual act, which is accompanied by pleasure, and the prophetic experience."

However, in several essays, Abulafia strives to clarify, as best as possible, the idea that pleasure itself constitutes the objective of the prophetic experience. In his book The Light of the Intellect, he writes:
"The letter is like matter, and the vocal-point is like the breath that moves this matter, and the understanding that functions and makes it function is like the intellect, and it is the intellect that operates on the breath and the matter; and the pleasure derived from everything that this combination enables to

achieve constitutes the true goal."

In his book The Treasure of Hidden Delights, he elaborates further:
"You will feel that a new breath will come to unite with you, awakening you and passing over your entire body. It will revitalize you, and you will have the impression that it pours over you, from head to feet, the oil of a perfumed balm, once or several times, and you will experience a feeling of contentment and great pleasure, a mixture of ecstatic joy and trembling, seizing both the soul and the body."

Thus, Abulafia was the first to consider physical pleasure as a means of expressing the sensation accompanying the prophetic experience, setting himself apart from other authors in whom the image of physical mating serves to describe their love for the divine.

CHAPTER IV
The Dialectic of the "I" and the "Nothing"

The Bible and the Talmud distinguish the "I" expressed as Ani (aleph-noun-yod) from another form of "I," expressed as Anokhi (aleph-noun-khaf-yod). These two terms refer to different modalities of the "I." The first, Ani, represents an "I" that is "in the process of becoming" through words. The second, Anokhi, refers to a fully realized "I," a definitive inscription in the Scriptures.

The Talmud explodes the term Anokhi and produces the phrase: Ana nafchi ketivat yahavit: "I, my soul, I give it to the writing." The difference between Ani and Anokhi is found in the letter Kaf, the first letter of the word ktav (writing). Kaf also means the palm of the hand.

In Kabbalistic texts, it is emphasized that the three letters composing the word Ani (aleph-noun-yod) also spell the word Ayin (aleph-yod-noun), meaning "nothing." Through the capacity to speak, the "I" (Ani) can experience the "nothing" (Ayin). In this sense, the "I" escapes any definition; this is its freedom, by which it distinguishes itself from all manufactured objects.

Objects are something, but the true "I," Ani, the properly human "I," is not something defined: it is not identifiable. In other words, it is a rupture with itself, for it transcends everything that could define it. The "I" (Ani) is distinguished by its refusal to assign an essence to itself, to be trapped in any definitive statement, or in any historical or natural definition. Ani embodies intrinsically Ayin, the "I" carries within itself the potentiality of "nothing." It is this ability to free itself from any mark of essence.

Fundamentally, it is a ma—a "What?" that diverts it from the risk of definition. The "man, what?" means that "it is characteristic of man not to have anything proper, his definition is not of having a definition, his essence is to have

119

no essence."

The "man, what?" is Ayin, nothing. It is impossible for him, if he desires to remain authentically human, to identify with any identity, whether natural, familial, or social. The characteristic of man is "nothing," freedom, ex-sistence, or transcendence. All these terms signify the ability to free oneself from the multiple codes that constantly threaten to imprison him.

The "man, what?" continuously risks becoming an "here is the man I am," confusing himself with particular determinations. He then becomes an "I-Anokhi," inscribed into an imaginary representation of himself. He accepts, often definitively, an image of himself; he identifies with a character or a role. By doing so, he ceases to be "nothing": he becomes something. Reified, re-identified, he loses the freedom that is constitutive of his humanity, of his authentic "I-Ani." He resolves to adhere to an image, abolishing the distance, the negation, the rupture, and, in fact, his potential to be different, which defined him as an ethical being and, above all, simply human.

The "I-Ani," which ex-sists in its capacity for liberation, refuses in its life the casual determination of consciousness and will through socio-economic relations that transform the subject's existence into an object or machine, whose gears and mechanisms could be disassembled.

The "I-Ani" refuses to be simply "the place," the "there" where Being would come to anchor and pass time; it is not, then, the place of destiny. It is not the passive being that lets itself be and succumbs to fate simply because it is "inscribed." Through its inventive action of "opposition," the "I-Ani" refuses the repetitive behavior or simply "already created" mode in which it would be limited to a mere plaything of nature or history. The "I-Ani" aims for humanity, not reification or animality; to achieve this, it becomes aware of its ability not to be closed upon itself as an object is.

The "I-Ani" is openness.

Openness governs, in a free being, the capacity to relate to what is and what is not, to impose limits defining what should and should not be. These limits are not of the absolute order, for, were they, upon reaching them, the death of the human being would ensue. The limits are strategically placed as "the Other, the other side." A duty to be different makes possible the power to be different.

When the "I" becomes Anokhi, it must, with all its strength, try to return to Ani-Ayin. It must aim for the "break," to explode the "I" that is identified, that has accepted the destiny of an identity. But the "break" can also become a system, and the "I" can then hide behind the image of the "Break," a condition that can be even more dangerous because in it, the self deceives itself about its existence.

Thus, it needs to aim for a "break of the break."

Meditation is this privileged moment in which the person frees themselves from their image of self, when they refuse to close themselves off in the maintenance of representation, in the abolition of time.

CHAPTER V
Energy, Shadow, and Disease

Meditation aims to direct existence toward physical and psychological well-being, acknowledging that the physical and psychological are deeply interdependent. Rabbi Nahman of Breslov explains in his book Liquoté Moharan the origins of disease.

For him, disease arises from an obstacle to the circulation of vital energy. The sick person is a being who is blocked, obstructed, chained, "closed." Therefore, healing consists of perceiving the knots that block the flow of this vital influx, which in Hebrew is called Chéfa (chin-phé-ayin).

It should be noted that when this word cannot be written in the order of its three letters (chin-phé-ayin), it can form (as a possibility) the word pécha (pé-chin-ayin), which means "lack" or "leak." This proximity is not meant to condemn the sick person, but rather to offer them the possibility of understanding that healing depends on them and their way of being in the world. The "lack" is not viewed in moral terms, but in existential terms.

Meditation seeks to bring to light the knots that obstruct the influx of energy and to untangle them, which would be done primarily by putting language into motion. Here is the full translation of an important passage from Rabbi Nahman. It is important to underline that the theological language he uses aims to translate a more ontological, existential language. The fundamental reading approach is to shift from a theological perspective to an anthropomorphic one:

"All of man's deficiencies—whether in children, work-salary, or health (banim, parnassa, and Beriyoute)—are characteristic of man himself. However, the light of the Holy One – blessed be He – continually pours upon him. It is the man himself, through his 'evil deeds,' who casts a shadow upon himself (tsel leatsmo), thus obstructing the light of God and preventing it from reaching him. The best way to eliminate the obstructing shadow is to annul oneself, to make oneself ayin."

With the clarification given in the previous chapter, the meaning of "making oneself ayin" is perfectly understood: it is a temporary nullification of one's "closed, heavy, and final identity" to rediscover the creative energy of becoming.

The energy that carries life is essentially temporal: it develops the time of the human.

Thus, every disease, as an obstruction to the passage of vital-temporal influx, is a "chronic" evil. The blockage of this influx blocks time, or perhaps it is more accurate to say that all factors that block temporality produce disease.

In Hebrew, the word for disease is mahala, derived from the root mahol, meaning "to make a circle," "to trace a circle." To get out of disease, one must exit the enclosure, the image of the circle, one must break the circle!

The corresponding relationship to the world is not a static given, a structured and determined set. On the contrary, it is a dynamic given, sliding through space and time. It is, in Heraclitus' image, a long river (rather calm). It is at once "past-present-future." Thus, the subject does not exist in a structured and determined whole.

Man, like reality, is in motion. Hebrew meditation essentially consists of perceiving this movement of being in order to internalize it and live.

For the Kabbalistic and Hasidic tradition, the light-influx of energy is found in a privileged way in the letters of the Hebrew alphabet and, more particularly, in the letters of the Divine Name. The placement of language into motion is thus the center of the meditative technique. Meditation is in a dynamic and energizing situation, a term which sometimes needs to be understood from both a concrete and symbolic point of view.

One of the essential aspects of the Hebrew rite is inscribing the marks of language in motion into reality, to remind man, the reader of the signs of the world, that he exists only in the dynamic of being.

The search for security led man to build structures in which he feels protected and, in which, he likes to establish himself as a center—at least to the extent that he can recognize such a center and identify with it. These structures are, moreover, necessary for the construction of personality, or according to our terminology, the Ani-Anokhi. However, settling into these determined structures is the greatest danger for the human.

Indeed, even if the "home," his "own house," the "community" offers a feeling of acceptance, belonging, and a viable structure to which he can identify and find his place, it is here that the problem arises.

The birth of a paradox: by identifying with the center of identity within the structure, he loses his own identity.

In the daily practice of life in society, this translates into affiliation with the "group," the "community," the "party," the "institution," the "ideology," the nation, etc., all of which require their members to adapt according to regulation, subordination.

The central identity of the group strips the members of their freedom, of their identity. The subject disappears into the anonymity of the group.

Hebrew meditation, linked to a hermeneutic practice, exploding the structures of the "already-there" of the institution, offers the subject the path to freedom. It opposes the rational construction of a "single-common subject," one that is subjected to the group, the state, the bureaucracy, the technocracy, and thus stripped of all individuality.

It is worth noting that numerous Hebrew rites consist precisely of exploding the structures of confinement. Whether it is the festival of Pessah (Passover), marking the liberation from slavery, or the festival of Soucot, which marks the stay in the desert (dwelling in temporary shelters to break free from the security that identifies the group), etc.

Ritual, then, is a way of aligning oneself with the dynamic vibrations of the influx of energy and allowing them to circulate in the human being. Any obstacle to this circulation of energy produces a knot or knots, which need to be untangled.

CHAPTER VI
Healing: Untangling the Knots
Meditation and Psychoanalysis

A passage from the Talmudic tractate Sanhedrin 100a will help us deepen our understanding of the disease-healing dialectic. In this text, the issue takes on the meaning of therapy and healing. Interestingly, although this may seem coincidental, the Hebrew term teroupha means healing. The phonetic similarity between terapia (therapy) and teroupha is more than a mere mnemonic device.

"Rabbi Yirmiya was sitting before Rabbi Zeïra and said: The Blessed Holy One will bring forth from the most holy of His abode a river; on the banks of this river will grow all kinds of delicious fruits, for it is written: 'And on the banks of the river, on both sides, will grow every kind of fruit tree, whose leaves will not wither and whose fruits will not fail. Every month, they will produce new fruits, for their waters flow from the sanctuary; their fruits will be for food and their leaves for medicine.' (Ezekiel 47:12)"

Rabbi Yirmiya emphasizes the prophecy of the prophet Ezekiel, which serves as the basis for the discussion among various Talmudic sages. What intrigues them in this verse is the phrase "and its leaves [will be] for medicine," which in Hebrew is written as Véa'léou literoupha. Rav Itshaq ben Abdimi and Rav Hisda have different comments on this point, but both agree that the word literoupha means "untangling." They break the word into two parts (in a "fragmented reading") and read it as lahatir pé — "to untangle the mouth."

For the Talmud, therapy is the "untangling," the "untying" of the mouth, and disease is the existence of a knot that functions as a lie and prohibition. The Hebrew word for "knot" is quécher, which is a variation of chéquer, meaning "lie." Lehatir means both "to untangle" and "to permit, authorize," the opposite of léessor, which means "to forbid." The central expressions in Halakha (Jewish law) are moutar (permitted)

126

and assour (forbidden), which can also be understood as "unbound" and "bound."

However, the two sages differ on the meaning of the "untying" of the mouth or, more specifically, its place of expression. Rav Itshaq ben Abdimi says it is the action of the "mouth from above" (pé chèl ma'ala), and Rav Hisda speaks of the "mouth from below" (pé chèl mata). Some see this as the mouth of speech, others as the mouth of sex or the womb. Ezekiel, in this context, views the leaves as a "remedy to untie the mouth of the mute," and Bar Kapaara sees them as "a remedy to open the womb of sterile women."

Rabbi Shmuel bar Nahmani says: "These leaves will serve to beautify the appearance of the speakers." He reads literoupha as letoar panim (to beautify the appearance) of the speakers.

What is this text teaching us? It teaches that disease is a "bad to be spoken" — using a Lacanian formulation in the entirely Talmudic sense. Disease is an inability to speak because the word is bound, because it no longer has space to express itself.

Rabbi Nathan of Nemirov, secretary and disciple of Rabbi Nahman of Breslov, emphasizes that the word alim, meaning "leaves," can refer both to "tree leaves" and to "pages of a book" or "written pages." "Pages of a book" to untangle, to liberate the bound word — this is the meaning of healing, the direction one must venture in order to erase the suffering of a "bad to be spoken."

A common pre-judgment sees analysis (a session of analysis) as a privileged moment during which a kind of hermeneutic genius allows the construction of interpretations of the most varied objects, reversals, imperfect acts, reunions, etc. Indeed, interpretation as an updating of meaning goes from a potential meaning to an actual one — this is a non-analysis. The Talmudic formula lehatir pé strongly emphasizes the aspect of "untangling."

Analysis, initially, is a "deconstruction" of meaning. The word in the session is not made to bring to light meanings but to introduce a "hole" (hor in Hebrew), which also means space (révah) and breath (rouah).

The therapeutic dimension of interpretation does not consist of semanticizing, of solidifying every listening of meaning. The "untangling" of lehatir pé nullifies the illusion in the patient and the analyst, who sees there a document to be decoded or "understood."

Thus, the danger of analyses in the fetishization of hermeneutics arises when analysis becomes about deciphering and elaborating meanings that trap the patient within the content of definitive consciousness, simultaneously nullifying the very sense of the analysis.

Analysis is a work of liberation and opening. This is the meaning of Rashi's comment that a bad dream is better than a good one because it disturbs and disrupts a state of satisfaction with a lethargic tendency. As a question, it breaks meaning instead of reinforcing it.

Interpretation in both analysis and the Talmud is stated in a paradox: "There is no construction except insofar as a deconstruction takes place." The work of interpretation inaugurates a work of "designification," of unreading, that opposes the semantic updating of words.

The therapy of teroupha works to "designify" the semantic fixations of language. Language, as a vehicle of meaning and tool of communication, uses a lexical system that assigns words an objective fixity of meaning, blocking language based on the conditions of discourse functionality.

The first moment of analysis is to reopen words to a polysemous functioning, and this leads to the rupture of an act of "designification," of "unreading," and untangling.

The essential application of Midrashic reading, but especially Kabbalistic reading, in the "reading of the letters" as opposed to the "reading of the words," is this deconstructive practice of language — a poetic practice of designification.

Designification frees all the constitutive elements of language: words no longer wish to mean "anything." But a novel lives and is created within the words themselves: syllables, consonants, and vowels begin to permute, to speak, to respond. They are made for exchange (and this process is a pleasure). There is a zero level of meaning, which is not the freezing of meaning but life, movement, and time.

Speaking in analysis is, through the power of disjunction and detachment (lehatir pé), opening the word through its emptiness. This opening is a renunciation and a detachment from the meanings in which the patient was trapped and understood themselves.

The zero level of meaning is just a moment between designification and resignification. It is an attempt to oppose meaning and, at the same time, to expose the very foundation of meaning.

The radical non-accumulation of meaning also raises a problem: either the disintegration of personality and, indeed, the impossibility of survival, or the systematization of the non-systematic, which amounts to sedimentation.

The pluralism of interpretation within the person themselves, as a dynamic play of different perspectives, seems to be a long-term solution.

Chapter VII: The Language of the Birds

160 For this approach to "analysis," we follow the texts of Nicolas Abraham, L'Écorce et le Noyau, Flammarion, 1987, Pierre Fédida, L'Absence, Gallimard, 1978, and Daniel Sibony, La Juive and Jouissance du dire, Grasset, 1983 and 1985.

The Teaching of Baal Shem Tov

The philosopher, fully aligned with the school of clear and distinct ideas, who seeks to maintain words in the precision of their meanings, who takes the words as a thousand small tools for lucid thought, cannot help but be astonished by the boldness of the Kabbalist, the man of the Midrash, or the Talmud. When studying the works of the Midrash, but even more so the Kabbalah and Hasidism, he will be surprised to find himself living in words, inside the words.

Kabbalistic and Hasidic reading creates new environments around and within words; it awakens hidden meanings that seemed crystallized into perfect solids.

The Bible, as a holy story, can describe to us, in a narrative reading, the story of a man named Noah who was saved from the flood by building an ark. Noah's Ark! The expression is well-known. All the animals of the earth are sheltered there (... except the fish), and a miniature world survived the destruction.

But what if Noah's Ark was not just a boat? What if the term "ark" meant something other than a kibotos in Greek, meaning "chest," or "ark" in Latin, meaning also "box" or "small chest"?

In Hebrew, the word that designates "Ark" is téva (tav-bèt-hé or tav-yod-bèt-hé). This term appears twice in the Bible: once during the episode of the Flood, and a second time during the birth of Moses, who was hidden in a téva on the waters of the Nile (Exodus, 2:5).

No one has ever spoken of the "Ark of Moses"! But much is said about a "holy Ark," even though in this case the Hebrew term is arone and not téva!

For the Hebrew, the term téva also means "word," as the Talmud indicates in this expression: téva bat chété otiyot, "a word of two letters," or the common expression: reché tévot, "heads of words," or "initials."

Baal Shem Tov picks up this polysemy of the word téva to produce a completely original reading of the Flood episode. To escape from the violence (hamass) mentioned in the text (Genesis, 6:18), it is not necessary to board a boat, but to enter into the "word" and there rediscover all dimensions and depths.

Violence would be a perversion of language that has lost the plural dimension it carries. It is quite surprising that the measurements of the "Ark" – 300 cubits for length, 50 for width, and 30 for height – write in Hebrew the word lachone (lamed = 30; chet = 300; nun = 50 [in gematria]), which means "language," sometimes the physical organ, but also the language of a country.

The analysis of the Ark's architecture teaches how a "language" and its element, the "word," must be built to exist in a language free from violence and destruction.

If we patiently revisit the biblical text and analyze it from this perspective, we will have taken a great step towards the study of Kabbalistic and Hasidic intuition. We will be able to penetrate the depth of every word and the heart of every Hebrew letter, which are themselves composed of words. The biblical text (Genesis, 6:14) says: "Make for yourself a téva."

Rabbi Levi Yitzhak of Berditchev explains that there are two types of relationships in language, one passive – using an already existing language to which man submits – and one active: "Man directs the letters." In this active relationship, man builds a new language that gives him a new vision of the world.

The opposition of the saying and the said, in the sense of Levinas, or the speaking word, spoken word of Merleau-Ponty.

To make the téva means to actively shape a language that speaks, that speaks to us. As Rabbi Kotzk says, it is not enough to penetrate the Talmud; it must also penetrate us.

We continue our reading of Noah's Ark by paying attention to the Midrash. In the same verse (Exodus, 6:14), we read: "[In the form] of nests you shall make the téva..."

What does the notion of "nest" mean in this context? What relation does language, the word, maintain with birds?

The Midrash Rabba is sensitive to this observation and offers an interpretation that supports our analysis. The Midrash says: "Just as the bird is atonement for the leper, so too the téva..." (Birds play a central role in the entire Flood story: the raven and the dove announced the reduction of the waters.)

The leper purification ceremony (Leviticus, 14) involves two birds, one of which is "sacrificed," and the other, after being dipped in the blood of the first, is released to freedom over the surface of the field (14:9).

The Midrash says: "Why does the purification of the leper depend on two pure birds? The voice comes to atone for the voice."

For the Midrashic and Talmudic tradition, leprosy (tsara'at) is a bodily affliction, the result of lashon hara, "slander," as it is more literally translated: "evil tongue," a bad relationship with language, a distortion of our inscription in words.

The Midrash preserves this idea by deriving the word metsora (leper) from a contraction of the expression motsi shem ra, meaning "one who brings forth an evil name"... This expression designates one who locks the other in a name or a non-viable category (ra), who assigns to them a final idea in order to dominate them, imprison them, and understand them. Violence consists of believing that man is a category like any other, an object manipulable and pledgable at will.

Violence is exercised against others, but also against oneself when one loses the ethical capacity for self-invention.

The Midrash gives a second explanation: the leper is one who has lost the sense of culpability and responsibility. The bird, in Hebrew tsipor (tsadé-pé-vav-réch), with its song, seeks to repair this situation. The word tsipor can also be read as tsérouf, meaning the "combination of letters of a word to produce other words," thus freeing or opening the elements of a structure to generate the possibility of the existence of other forms.

But the tsipor, the bird, has an even more essential meaning: it is the very metaphor for the relationship between language and the real, the ability to introduce into the material world a word that makes it live and sets it in motion.

Indeed, the word tsipor is composed of the term tsour ("rock") and pé ("mouth"): literally, a bird in Hebrew is a "mouth" within a "rock"...

The fundamental idea of all Kabbalistic thought: to inscribe language in the real world, is even present in the first covenant, which marks words on the body; this is precisely the meaning of circumcision, mila in Hebrew, which means "word," synonymous with téva.

For Kabbalistic and Hasidic thought, all words find their origin and power of meaning in the word of words: the Name of God.

The bird, in the sense of "mouth in the rock," is, in a way, a paradigm of the structure of the ritual that consists of rediscovering the divine Names interwoven in the real world to give ritual gestures and words a dimension in harmony with the infinite.

The place of the ritual experience is the "Land of Israel": this idea is discovered in reverse, in the interstices of two important events in the biblical narrative. Moses does not step onto the soil of Israel because of a single fault: he had struck the rock instead of speaking to it. We will discover a new aspect of Moses' personality that is not surprising, since he, like Noah, was one of the only ones to have been in a téva.

Moses' greatness is, at the same time, a "weakness": his world is not the real everyday world. His words do not adhere to reality. For him, every word is a suffering, a kind of failure between words and things; language that neither designates nor exposes. Hence, an anomaly of the word, which popular vision has interpreted as a stutter.

This radical impossibility for Moses to inscribe the words, the names/the Divine Name in the real world, explains this astonishing passage where he fails to circumcise Eliezer, his second son (Exodus 4:24-26). A tremendous humor in the text places the action in a malon, a word that means both "inn" and "dictionary" or "place of circumcision"...

Moses, "the uncircumcised of the lips" (arel séfatai), finds himself on the path in an "inn-dictionary-place of circumcision," and God touches him and wishes to make him die. A dramatic turn!

It is Tsipora, Moses' wife, who takes a piece of rock, tsour, and performs the circumcision of Eliezer.

Tsipora! Whose name precisely means the birdcatcher and whose letters of the name fit into pé in tsour, "the mouth of the rock"...

Moses will not enter the Land of Israel because he never succeeded in "descending" to the level of humans and a mundane reality that should necessarily have been penetrated by a "word-name."

Moses, in Hebrew Moshé, mem-chin-hé, is written with three letters that also write the word "name." Moses is the name. His coming into the world passes through the téva. He enters the word; he will be saved to play an important political role and guide the people, but his uncircumcision of the lips, which perhaps indicates a lack of life in language, will never allow him to experience the land.

A parallel passage in the biblical account confirms our analysis. The 13th chapter of the Book of Numbers recounts the episode of the explorers; Moses sends twelve explorers to "spy out" the land of Israel before entering it. All return with a grandiloquent description: everything there is great, the fruits of the land and of the people. The explorers inspire fear and despair in the hearts of the children of Israel. The entire desert generation will die in the desert, slowly, over forty years. Death caused by the sin of the explorers.

But what sin? Was it because they told the truth about the situation of the land? Was it because they allowed the belief that a situation is final and unchangeable? Was it because they perceived and offered the world in a logic of identity, forgetting the dimension of life as future, change, and alternation?

The sin of the explorers is that they forgot that existence is a "battle" against the given being, to create new situations: the fundamental plasticity of being. This is the meaning of Israel's very name, which Jacob acquired during his struggle with the man (Genesis 32): "Your name shall no longer be Jacob, but Israel, for you have struggled with God and with men..."

To be, for man, is to be willing to be.

135

The Kabbalistic and Hasidic vision embraces the possibility of this incessant future, in the way of living language in its relation to the real world. Words are nothing but tools for designation that give access only to things; they are also the life of things and our life in things if we know how to understand the vibrations of life that penetrate matter.

This vibration of life is, for Kabbalists, the very Name of God, the Tetragrammaton, formed of four consonants without vowels, which is inscribed in the matter of the world and whose ritual consists of rediscovering existence. This commentary helps us understand the meaning of a paradigmatic ritual presented in a biblical text as tiqqun, that is, "repair," for the sin of the explorers. In chapter 15, verse 37 of the Book of Numbers, God speaks to Moses in these terms:

"Speak to the children of Israel: you shall make a tsitsit [fringe] on the corners of your garments for your generations. And you shall put a thread of blue at the edge of the tsitsit (fringes). And this shall be to you for a tsitsit, and you shall see it and remember all the commandments of the Lord Y-h-v-h and do them, and you shall not turn aside your hearts and eyes as you have done until now."

This text constitutes the thirtieth part of the most well-known text in the Jewish tradition, entitled the Shema Israel, which consists of the following three passages: Deuteronomy 6:4-9; Deuteronomy 11:13-21, and Numbers 15:37-41.

From this text in the Book of Numbers, we learn the mitsva of the tsitsit: a ritual consisting of wearing a garment with four corners called tallit, upon which threads are attached with knots in such a way that the number of knots and turns corresponds numerically to the Name of God.

From this text in the Book of Numbers, we learn the mitzvah of the tsitsit: a ritual that involves wearing a garment with four corners called a tallit, to which threads are attached with knots in such a way that the number of knots and loops corresponds numerically to the Name of God. This exemplary ritual is the inscription of the "word in the rock," the bird, the inscription of the Name in the matter (the garment). In the text, the bird is not forgotten. An allusion to it is made through the word "corner," which is kanaf and also means "wing of a bird."

The text explicitly states that this ritual allows one to remember all the mitzvot, all the other rituals, because here we have a particularly clear case of the meaning of the ritual: seeing in the real world the vibrations of the Name.

Thus, we understand a Talmudic text that says the tsitsit ritual is equivalent to all other mitzvot of the Torah (Ménahot 43b, Nédarim 25a, and Chevouot 29a). This doesn't mean that simply wearing a tallit is enough to fulfill all other rituals, but the most fundamental teaching is that the analysis of the tallit-tsitsit ritual teaches us the general meaning, the nodal structure, of all rituals.

Rashi comments: the numerical value (gematria) of the word tsitsit is 600 (tsadé-yod-tsadé-yod-tav = 90+10+90+10+400). One must count the 5 knots and 8 threads, making a total of 613, which is the total number of mitzvot—365 negative and 248 positive. What is Rashi trying to teach? Is he, the rationalist, commenting on the Talmud linearly and literally, "delirious"? What need does he have to provide a numerical value that, in fact, explains nothing and merely reinforces the Talmudic observation? He rephrases, in another way, the equivalence of the tsitsit with all other mitzvot!

In reality, his comment doesn't reside in the numerical equivalence, but in the need, to produce this gematria, to compute the numerical value of the words, knots, and threads (600 of the word, 13 of the knots and threads); the necessity to mix, through the meaning of the ritual, the matter of words and the matter of things. The intertwining of matter and the "word-Name-of-God" is the very meaning of the entire Hebrew ritual.

By completing it through a ritual gesture, the Jew creates this junction of the real and the language, and "branches out" over

the Infinite of the Name, which is not just a word but the very
energy of language and of the word.

This entanglement of the thing and the Name is part of a
specific metaphor, that of the bird. We will discover there
a methodological tool of great importance: whenever we
encounter the idea of the bird, it will be the subject of the
adventures of the ritual, its difficulties, failures, distortions,
perversions, or successful assumptions.

CHAPTER VIII

A Mysticism of Letters in Motion

The preceding chapters have helped us understand the necessity of a language in motion, one that allows the "man of word" to remain in the uninterrupted flow of being. The Kabbalists and the masters of Hasidism have adopted this idea in its most concrete sense and have developed a set of systems that place language in motion.

For the Kabbalistic and Hasidic tradition, the matter of the world rests upon the structure of the Hebrew alphabet.

The Hebrew language is one of direct adhesion to matter, space, and time. Its words, sounds, and the materiality of the forms of its letters marry the contours and rhythms of the world and creation.

Hebrew is the geography (writing of the land) and the geometry (measure of the land) of the created.

Hebrew is read in the very reliefs of matter; every object within it is a sound; a letter, a term, resembling the solid character of Hebrew writing, with its roots, its thickness, and the abrupt roughness of meaning.

As the Sepher Yetzira (the Book of Formation) teaches: "By 32 paths the world was created, by 10 primordial numbers and 22 fundamental letters."

The Sepher Yetzira then studies in detail the relationship between the letters and the body, which we will analyze later. Rabbi Abraham Abulafia, whom we spoke of earlier, proposes a system of meditation based on the Hebrew alphabet. Every person has a potential that allows him to reach high levels of consciousness, sometimes approaching prophecy. For Abulafia, the letters of the Hebrew alphabet are a real path to the sacred source within us, enabling us to elevate ourselves to the world of transcendence.

The core of the Hebrew language is the Tetragrammaton YHVH, from which all other names and words derive. Among the Hasidic masters, Kabbalistic meditation is repeated and transmitted secretly from master to disciple. This is one reason for its apparent non-existence. This meditation technique, which recalls certain techniques of yoga, makes use, as we will see, of body postures, breathing techniques, visualization, and chanting. Before presenting these techniques, it is first necessary to understand the deep structure of the Hebrew language and of the Tetragrammaton YHVH, the basis for the exercises we will propose.

In the beginning, there was the point...

In the Kabbalistic structure, before the play of words, before the use of polysemy and semantic energy, there is the form of the letters: a graphical, pictorial view of the alphabet.
What is a letter of the alphabet?
It is, at first, a sign that designates a certain sound — in linguistics, it would be called a phoneme. An organized set of phonetic signs constitutes a word, which also has its global equivalent in sound, its pronunciation.
The letter is created by man for a specific purpose: to construct, with the help of other letters, the words of the language, which, in turn, serve as vehicles for ideal significations such as "cat," "door," "circle," etc.
But it is possible to disregard this purpose of the letter, no longer seeing it as a letter, but rather as a simple form, a certain graphic design composed of various segments of varied orientations.
When the linguistic purpose of the letter disappears or is set aside, it no longer remains a letter but becomes a graphic form.
A decisive event then occurs. In the presence of this letter, which has just been stripped of its function as a letter (which is to belong to the system of language), the observer experiences a new feeling, different from what was felt in front of the ordinary letter.
The emergence of an unknown form, derived from the known letter, but never before perceived in its purity and formal autonomy, provokes new impressions, even new emotions.
And this is true both for the overall shape of the letter and the linear segments that compose it. There is an effort of "deconstruction" of a phenomenological type in the sense

that it is necessary to rediscover, under the sedimentation of the habitual meaning that has dulled the vision, the living meaning, a strong and deep tone.

But the Kabbalist and the master of the Midrash or Talmud do not think that their "designifying" reading leads to the purity of the meaning, the only true one. The effective event that is revealed, the new tonalities of things, is still an interpretation, nothing more than an interpretation.

Even though some Kabbalists have been able, through this "designification," or Tsimtsum of the spirit, to feel and understand in themselves the whisper of the absolute, without it being a particular and resumed form of the world, it is still within a radical subjectivity that all these new tonalities appear.

The aleph is not blue for everyone, and the reish or the yod are not happier or sadder than other letters. Moreover, experience and situational motivations are the sources of interpretations. We want to indicate, by these observations, that an essential moment in the experience of Kabbalistic reading passes through a deformation, a rupture of classical perception, which provokes a sense of strangeness, unease, perhaps discomfort.

But there is no access to a meaning that was already present under the sedimented bed of meaning. The Kabbalistic reading acts to reconstruct new meanings, to unveil new tonalities that escape the stereotyped and weakened significations of the everyday world. There are, therefore, no pre-fabricated grids of interpretations for graphic forms. This means that the interpretations one may find in this or that Kabbalist or those we ourselves may give, are not interpretations that claim any universal or absolute validity. Rabbi Ichaya Horowitz explains, in his book Chené Louhot HaBerit (The Two Tablets of the Covenant), the process of creation of the world in relation to the letters of the Hebrew alphabet and particularly with those of the Tetragrammaton: yod-he-vav-he.

In the beginning, there is beriya, that is, literally, creation, the passage from absolute nothingness to being, the passage from Ayim to Yèch, constituting the raw material of the universe, which is called in biblical Hebrew Tohou, and in the Midrashic language évène chetiva, meaning the "cornerstone." This is precisely why, in philosophical Hebrew, derived from Greek, this raw material is called héyouli, that is, hyle material.

This raw material, the infinitesimal element of matter, is the point.

Creation (beriya) designates the birth of this point of matter, which was perceived in Antiquity as that which could not be reduced to a smaller element and was called the atom (from the Greek: indivisible).

If we use physics as a metaphor to describe the creation of the world, we must say that the point of matter, the smallest particle discovered to date, is called a "quark," according to a mysterious quote by James Joyce.

"In the beginning, therefore, there was the point..." The passage from non-visible non-being to visible being, a threshold, a frontier, the infinitesimal emergence of being. It is necessary to understand the point not in a static perspective but as the dynamic and balanced result of a set of contradictory forces: forces of retention and concentration and forces of expansion.

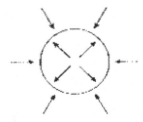

The Metamorphoses of the Point

The second phase of creation is called yetsira: the "formation."
Here, the infinite metamorphoses of the point occur, driven by
the interplay of forces that come into play.

For the masters of Kabbalah, the first transfiguration of the
point is a vertical line, whose birth supports various possible
explanations.

It could be that an internal force within the point becomes
stronger than an external force, thus making the expansion of
the point possible.

If the force F2, previously in equilibrium with F1, disappears
for various reasons, the point can then extend:

If we consider that the definition of the line is a displacement
of the point, then the line will be the result of a "battle"
between the forces of the point and other forces trying to move
it. In our case, it is the action of superior forces coming from

above:
In this third hypothesis, one or two forces may intervene. The particular shape of the line will be the result.

The shape produced by a single force acting constantly on this point is a line that extends indefinitely in the same direction, that is, a straight line. The movement results from the fact that a shape has been subjected to the concentric tension of the point, causing it to shift indefinitely in a constant direction.

In the second case, the linear shape results from the combined action of two forces. This situation unfolds depending on whether the intervention of the two forces is simultaneous or successive.
Simultaneous action creates a curved line.
Successive action creates an angular or broken line.

The inflection of the curve will depend on the strength of the lateral force in relation to the force that, acting only on the point, would produce a straight line.
Likewise, the length of each of the segments forms a broken line attributed to the time during which each of the forces acts, while the nature of the angle, which abruptly alters the trajectory, is the effect of the intensity of the force that comes into play when the first one stops.

To this vertical line, the birth of a horizontal line is added according to the same process, and thus the plane is born. Thus we have:

The point;
The line (vertical);
The plane.

CHAPTER IX
Gematria
Geometry and Semantic Energy

For the masters of Kabbalah, these three primordial geometric forms are the origin of the Hebrew alphabet.

All the letters would be constructed from a combination of the point, the line, and the plane, which become the three fundamental letters of the alphabet: yod, vav, and dalet.

Indeed, the letter yod is a point, the letter vav is a vertical line, and the dalet is a plane.

Thus, the first letter of the alphabet, aleph, is "the first letter constructed." It is composed of the three letters yod-vav-dalet, with the line of the vav inclined to the left. [Let us remember that Hebrew is written from right to left, unlike Portuguese, for example.]

Then, the letters were stylized, rounded or angled according to different traditions.

Each letter has a graphic form that is soundless. The letters belong to pure visibility. To pronounce or name them, it is necessary to unfold them using other consonant and vowel letters.

For example, the letter ◎ (Aleph) is seen but not pronounced. To name it, one must add a ◎ (Lamed) and a ◎ (Peh). From a phonetic point of view, it is read as "alèph," with the vowel being "è." Some letters have a variable unfolding, while others can be written in different forms.

Thus, we note in essence that the letter yod, or the point, unfolds into yod-vav-dalèt, meaning point-line-plane.

This geometric view of the alphabet is what is properly called guématria, a Hebrew term derived from the Greek, meaning geometry. Later on, the word guématria took on the meaning of numerical equivalence, the relationship between numbers and letters, which we will refer to as "semantic energy" or "semantic force."

The Semantic Energy

Each Hebrew letter has a numerical value or semantic energy that must be understood in order to comprehend Hebrew texts.
The alphabetic numbering system is based on the decimal system. It involves using the 22 consonant letters of the alphabet, associating them in the following order:

The first nine letters are associated with the simple units (1 to 9);
The next nine letters correspond to the tens (10, 20, 30, etc.);
The last four letters correspond to the numbers 100, 200, 300, and 400.

Lettres hébraïques	Noms et transcriptions des lettres		Valeurs numériques	Lettres hébraïques	Noms et transcriptions des lettres		Valeurs numériques
				כ	KAF	k	20
				ל	LAMÈD	l	30
א	ALEPH	'a	1	מ	MÊM	m	40
ב	BÊT	b	2	נ	NOUN	n	50
ג	GUIMÈL	g	3	ס	SAMÈKH	s	60
ד	DALÈT	d	4	ע	'AYIN	'	70
ה	HÉ	h	5	פ	PÉ	p	80
ו	VAV	v	6	צ	TSADÉ	ts	90
ז	ZAYIN	z	7	ק	QOF	q	100
ח	HÈT	h	8	ר	RÈCH	r	200
ט	TÈT	t	9	ש	CHIN	ch	300
י	YOD	y	10	ת	TAV	t	400

There are five final letters with the following values:

Final kaf = 50
Final mem = 600
Final nun = 700
Final pe = 800
Final tsade = 900

In the Hebrew language, there is a kind of weighted vision of the letters: a reading and even a vowel has a weight of significance. Words that are composed of the same letters, even though they have completely different meanings, even opposites, are related to one another. For example, the word for salt, mélah, is related to the word for dream, halom—both of these words are composed of the same three letters, mem-

147

het-lamed, in a different order. Their "semantic energy" is the same; the difference in meaning lies in the sequence of the letters.

This process of combination, which we will return to in more detail, is called tsérouf.

This idea of "semantic weight" helps better understand guématria. It is a "semantic energy" resulting from the sum of the letters of a word. Thus, two different words, which do not have the same letters but whose numerical value is identical, share the same "semantic energy."

In most cases, the ritual consists of playing with this energy, not only at the level of words but in their translation into the real world. The ritual, in a way, inscribes language into the real world, which is the first moment of a more essential purpose. The ritual frees the closed structure of mundane reality through the combinatorial freedom of the letters it carries.

CHAPTER X
The Tetragram
Geometric Vision

The masters of Kabbalah, in order to understand the numerical value of the letters, approach the Tetragram through two main axes: guématria, that is, the graphic form of the letters, and their semantic energy.

The observations from the previous chapters help us better understand the meaning of the Tetragram.
It consists of four consonants without vowels: yod-hé-vav-hé ⊚⊚⊚⊚, which we transliterate as Y-H-V-H.

Where does this Name come from?
According to Rabbi Ichaya Horowitz, it is the result of the story of the primordial point and its metamorphoses.
The "point-yod" becomes "line-vav" and "plane-dalèt": three graphic forms that the letter yod itself writes in its unfolded script.

The development of the point, in its specificity as a Hebrew letter, invites us to understand, even if intuitively, through what path and thanks to which mediations the simple spatiality transforms "the" pragmatic space into "symbolic" space. For there is a great distance from the primordial emptiness of space to the formed space, a distance that conditions the intuition of objects according to a particular modality. There is no space with absolute value. Simple spatiality becomes "the" space through a particular injection of meanings that is unique to each culture. The "here" and the "there," the "high" and the "low," acquire specific determinations which, in turn, model "the" space.

This relationship between the Name and Hebrew space is formulated very precisely in Kabbalah, through an author like Gikatilla, for example. The Tent of Meeting, the Ohel Moed, and, later, the Temple of Solomon are spaces for receiving the Name. This translates as follows: it is the names themselves that constitute space, the different spaces of the Temple. To trace the Name is to divide a space into different places and construct "the" particular space in which consciousness will establish a determined point of view on the world, a spiritual reference system.

The space formed by the Name first refers to a transcendence, an essential "far away." Gikatilla observes this semantic duality of the word cham, which means both "Name" and "far away."
"The root of the word 'Name' [Chém] comes from the term 'far away' [Cham]. Every time there is 'Name,' there is also 'far away,' and vice versa."

An essential observation concerning the reflection on identity: the Name confers a certain identity upon the one who bears it. To say that the "Name" is the "far away" leads back to the paradox of an identity that is constructed by undoing itself, in a kind of constant disidentification.

Thus, the first letter of the Tetragram cuts the primary spatiality into a particular space, the graphic form of which the letters developed there invite us to discover. The primordial "point," in its extreme conciseness, in its concentric tension, is the mark of contraction, the Tsimtsoum that created a matricial space, which is, in itself, the opposite of the creator. This space of opposition is so important that some commentators of Rabbi Itshaq Louria, like Rabbi Nahman of Braslav, boldly claim that the empty space left by the Tsimtsoum is a space "empty of God."

The theological is an ontological contradiction in itself. Thus, to speak of God in this world is to assert the impossibility of His presence. The world is the radical contraction of God.

However...

However, it must also be asserted at the same time that "there is" and "there is no" God. An ontological contradiction whose resulting tensions are, to a large extent, creators of life.

The "point," as the paradoxical presence of a being that is both present and absent at the same time, is the leveling of forces between "being" and "non-being." Being and non-being at the same time, this is the question on which the world rests.

Hebrew grammar has preserved this contradiction and question that marks the point in vav for the dual grammatical function of this letter.

Indeed, vav is grammatically vav hahibour, a coordinating conjunction, and vav hahipoukh, a prefix that inverts the temporality of the verb. By placing vav before a past tense, the verb becomes future, and conversely: placed before a future, vav turns it into a past. This mutation of tenses is also a challenge to human logic, because time is linear and inevitably flows from the present to the future.

If it were necessary to characterize vav in one word, we would say it denotes metaphysics, in the sense of a relationship between the "creator" and the "creature."

The third phase is the writing of dalèt:

A new dimension "of" space appears here. After the metaphysical relation, which is marked by the verticality of the vav, a horizontal relationship is drawn: that of man with another man, which we will qualify, borrowing the terminology of Levinas, as an ethical relationship.

The letter dalèt in Hebrew means door, dalèt. A simple

observation, but one that will allow us, as we will see, to understand numerous biblical passages. In our interpretation, it means that "access to" always passes through a dual dimension: metaphysical and ethical.

If we translate these ideas into Hasidic language, that is, if we existentialize them and thus step outside the theological sphere, the primordial "point" becomes the proper place of the human, where necessarily, a door opens onto an existence, simultaneously toward the world, God, and the other.

CHAPTER XI
The Cave of Makhpela
Ancestral Memory

According to Rabbi Itshaq Louria, the two letters hé that make up the Tetragrammaton are letters composed of different elements. He calls this unfolding of the hé: the Cave of Makhpela, a name that literally means: the unfolding of the letter hé.

The hé can be written in two forms. It is composed either of a dalèt and a vav:

...or it is composed of a dalèt and a yod:

Thus, the Tetragrammaton would be the development of the yod: yod-vav-dalèt, in two different forms, in two different combinations.

One of these would result in the sequence: yod-dalèt-vav, and the other would result in: vav-dalèt-yod. The primordial point would then, initially, become a hé composed of a dalèt and a vav, which would give the sequence yod-dalèt-vav:

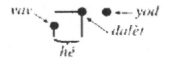

Then, the yod would fracture into the sequence vav-dalèt-yod:

Thus, the Tetragrammaton would be the explosion of the point into two points that would develop in two opposite forms.

The Tetragrammaton in motion begins from the point and returns to it.

Kabbalah does not reside in the knowledge of these facts. Knowledge can be acquired as information, but the sage is not necessarily a Kabbalist... Kabbalah is an experience, not just knowledge. It is beyond knowledge...

Knowing the graphical structure of the Tetragrammaton has no value except in the transmission of this information through a meditative and active experience.

The name YHVH, given as visible by four consonants without vowels, is ineffable. A name that was made to be hidden, as the Talmud says. It should not be read as léolam ("eternal"), but léélem ("to conceal it").

The Name hides itself at the same time it reveals itself. An essential paradox that affirms an irreducible relationship between God and the knowledge that thematizes, defines, or synthesizes. Through this retraction in silence, revelation preserves the transcendence of what it manifests.

The absence of vowels, which makes the Name unpronounceable, creates an insurmountable distance that removes the possibility of taking God as an object.

The Tetragrammaton is also a gap in language, from which language itself takes meaning.

CHAPTER XII
The Semantic Energy of the
Variations of the Tetragrammaton

The Jewish ritual is, for the Kabbalists, a way of writing the Name into the matter of the world, a way of living in the space of the Name.

In the previous chapter, we sought to highlight how the Talmudists, Midrashists, and Kabbalists lived the language, how they marked and engraved it into the objects of the world, and how they released the language through a succession of explosions until the discovery of the "primordial point." In this process, we first highlighted the semantic point of view: a term has meaning through the set of letters that compose it. The cut, the "explosion" of the term into two terms, or the combination of letters with one another, form the sources of new words or expressions.

In the second moment, we revealed in the letters, and especially in those of the divine Name, the possibility of a graphic reading that abstracts the semantic meaning to retain only the fragment of a space and the metamorphoses of forms such as the point, the line, or the surface.

Immediately, we observed that no reading is exclusive and that it is possible to use them together or separately.

On the path of the "explosion," it was quickly verified that the semantic and graphic levels still did not offer enough opening. Thus, the masters of Hebrew thought, in order to pursue the necessary rupture that would bring them closer to infinity, made use of a third way. This third way is the most well-known, already approached in these pages. It uses the "value of the numerical," a procedure that we prefer to call "semantic energy."

The Tetragrammatic Name will unfold into four Names, each representing a different modality of the perception of the divine by man, a different experience of transcendence.

To understand these four Names and their constitution, it is necessary to add details about the way Hebrew letters are written. Each letter has a graphic form that is soundless. The letters belong to pure visibility. To pronounce them, to name them, it is necessary to unfold them using other consonants and vowels.

For example, the aleph is seen but not pronounced. To name it, it is necessary to join a lamed and a phé. Thus, it is read aleph. The vowel is "e."

Some letters have an invariable unfolding, others can be written in different forms. Regarding the Tetragrammaton, it is composed of four consonants, two of which are identical: the hé. There are, therefore, three different consonants: the yod, the hé, and the vav.

The yod is invariable and is always written: yod-vav-dalèt.

The hé can be written in three forms:

hé-yod (yod index)
hé-aleph (aleph index)
hé-hé (duplicated)
Likewise, the vav can be written in three ways:

vav-yod-vav (yod index)
vav-aleph-vav (aleph index)
vav-vav (duplicated)
Starting from these variations, the Kabbalists and, in particular, the school of Safed, with Rabbi Itshaq Louria and his disciples, officially retained four Names.

In the following different analyses, the numerical value of each letter also intervenes. The first Name, called "Chem av," is the unfolding of the Tetragrammaton using the letters in their "yod index" writing, which results in:

$$\left.\begin{array}{l} \textit{yod: yod-vav-dalèt} \\ \textit{hé: hé-yod} \\ \textit{vav: vav-yod-vav} \\ \textit{hé: hé-yod} \end{array}\right\} \quad \text{10 letras}$$

The numerical value of this Name is:

$$
\begin{array}{lr}
10 + 06 + 04 = & 20 \\
05 + 10 \quad\;\; = 15 & \\
06 + 10 + 06 = & 22 \\
\underline{05 + 10 \quad\;\; = 15} & \\
\text{Total} & 72
\end{array}
$$

The Name consists of 10 letters in its unfolding and has a total numerical value of 72. 72 is said in Hebrew as ayin-bet or av, from where the expression: Name of av or Chem av.

The second Name, called "Chem sag."

The second Name is the unfolding of the Tetragrammaton using the hé in its "yod index" writing and the vav in its "aleph index" writing.

$$\left.\begin{array}{l} \textit{yod: yod-vav-dalèt} \\ \textit{hé: hé-yod} \\ \textit{vav: vav-aleph-vav} \\ \textit{hé: hé-yod} \end{array}\right\} \quad \text{10 letras}$$

The numerical value of this Name is:

10 + 06 + 04 =	20
05 + 10 =15	
06 + 01 + 06 =	13
05 + 10 =	15
Total	63

This Name is composed of 10 letters and has a numerical value of 63, in Hebrew samekh-guimel or sag, from which the expression Chem sag comes.

The third Name, called "Chem ma"

The third Name is a development of the Tetragrammaton that uses the letters in their "aleph index."

yod: yod-vav-dalèt
hé: hé-aleph
vav: vav-aleph-vav
hé: hé-aleph

} 10 letras

The numerical value of this Name is:

10 + 06 + 04 =	20
05 + 01 =	06
06 + 01 + 06 =	07
05 + 01 =06	
Total	45

The Name is composed of 10 letters and has a numerical value of 45, in Hebrew mèm-hé or ma, from which the expression Chem ma comes.

The fourth Name, called "Chem ben."

The fourth Name is the development of the Tetragrammaton that uses the letters in their "duplicated index," which gives:

$$yod: yod\text{-}vav\text{-}dal\grave{e}t$$
$$h\acute{e}: h\acute{e}\text{-}h\acute{e}$$
$$vav: vav\text{-}vav$$
$$h\acute{e}: h\acute{e}\text{-}h\acute{e}$$

$\left.\right\}$ 9 letras

It has a numerical value of:

10 + 06 + 04 =		20
05 + 05	=	10
06 + 06	=12	
05 + 05	=10	
Total		52

This Name consists of 9 letters and has a numerical value of 52, in Hebrew: noun-bèt, which is pronounced nav or ben, from where the expression Chem ben.

CHAPTER XIII
The Journey of the Names

The mystical experience is based on a relationship with language, with the Hebrew letters, as a language in movement, the literal vehicle of being. As we said earlier, a "language in movement" is needed for a "man in movement." The alphabet is the series of 22 consonants: aleph, bét, guimel, etc. If we put the alphabet in motion, each letter becomes the next. Thus, aleph becomes bét, bét becomes guimel, and so on. When we apply this procedure to the Tetragrammaton:

the yod becomes kaf;
the hé becomes vav;
the vav becomes zayin;
the hé becomes vav.

$$\text{YHVH} \longrightarrow \text{KVZV.}$$

The KVZV can be pronounced "kouzou" – the vav, used as the vowel "chourouq," is pronounced as "ou."
Although this name is not well-known, it is perhaps one of the most widespread in Jewish practice, as it appears at the heart of the Jewish ritual of the mezuzah. This ritual involves placing a scroll on the right side of each significant door in the house, with the first two passages of the Shema Yisrael written on the scroll.

When the scroll is rolled up with the writing inside, two Names must be written on the exterior. One is right-side up, and the other is inverted, so that the scroll must be turned to read it. The right-side-up Name is Chadaï, and the inverted Name is kouzou bemoukhsaz kouzou.

The entire scroll is called the mezuzah, a word that comes from the root "lazouz," meaning "to move, to set in motion." The fundamental experience of the journey is one that the person must mark on the door of the house so as not to forget that, despite staying within four walls, the journey still awaits them.

The movement and the path are not only inscribed in the word mezuzah but also in this writing in motion that is required for the Name kouzou.

According to Gikatilla, kouzou is a commentary on the phrase "Hear, O Israel, YHVH is our God, YHVH is One."
He says:
"Whenever the Tetragrammaton is found, it means to say the Tetragrammaton is One [YHVH EHAD], and this is the secret of the Celestial Chariot [sod maassé merkava]. The Tetragrammaton in the action of the chariot is kouzou. And the secret of kouzou is YHVH EHAD, God is One."

Two important concepts appear in this text. The first is a new and original explanation of the Celestial Chariot. The word merkava would be derived from the root leharkiv, which means to make ride. In French, "faire cavalier" (to make ride, overlay) of two letters or two words is "inserting" them. The process of moving letters would proceed from the merkava, or inversely, the merkava would be the language in motion.

The second important concept tells us that the two words YHVH EHAD have the same numerical value as the word kouzou:

YHVH = 26, EHAD = 13, KOUZOU = 39.
The One God is the Tetragrammatic God whose letters move.

The "One Tetragram" is not the absolute of an immovable identity, but the differentiation of itself within itself. The "oneness of the Name" is the possibility of internal distancing that produces life itself. Even God, in His oneness, is not identity. Gikatilla summarized this as follows: "The words 'God' and 'God is One' mean: the Name in movement."

YHVH = YHVH EHAD = KOUZOU

It is this fundamental idea of language in movement that gives birth, in Kabbalah, to a set of processes of unfolding the Name and analyzing its numerical values or semantic energies. Here, we will study the main unfoldings of the Tetragrammaton Name. However, it is important to clarify that merely possessing knowledge about these different techniques is not enough to be considered a Kabbalist.

The objective of these unfoldings is to guide various meditation experiences or indicate, whenever necessary, the meaning of the forces at play in this or that phenomenon.

When commenting on verse 15 of the third chapter of Exodus, "This is my Name forever, and this will be my mention for all generations," the Talmud explains that the Name is the Tetragrammaton YHVH, which we will call Chem-Havaya, and that the mention of the Name is the Name of the Name, which we will call Chem-Adnout, written aleph-dalèt-noun-yod.

The Name, in its duality, carries, in miniature, the duality of the Written Torah and the Oral Torah. There is the ineffable Written Name: YHVH (Chem-Havaya). There is the pronounced Name, which is written ADNY (Cham-Adnout).

The semantic energy of Chem-Havaya (YHVH) is 26.

$$
\left.
\begin{array}{lcl}
yod & = & 10 \\
h\acute{e} & = & 05 \\
vav & = & 06 \\
h\acute{e} & = & 05
\end{array}
\right\} \quad 10 + 05 + 06 + 05 = 26.
$$

The Chem-Adnout is called the "Palace of the Name" (Hékhal). It has a numerical value of 65: aleph-dalèt-noun-yod: $1 + 4 + 50 + 10$.

Verse 20 of chapter 2 of the prophet Habakkuk provides a clue of astonishing clarity. It says: "But YHVH is in His holy temple (hékhal); let all the earth be silent before Him."

In Hebrew, the expression "be silent before Him" is said as: has mipanav. The word silence (has) is written hé-samékh and has a numerical value of 65, just like the word hékhal (hé-yod-kof-lamed: $5 + 10 + 20 + 30$).

This verse from Habakkuk is a true Kabbalistic equation that can be read as: YHVH in the Hékhal, whose numerical value is 65 (which corresponds to Chem-Adnout).

In fact, there is a third Name frequently used, which is ELOHIM, whose semantic energy is 86.

Aleph	= 01
Lamed	= 30
Hé	= 05
Yod	= 10
Mèm	= 40

01+30+05+10+40 = 86

CHAPTER XV

The Tsérouf: The Art of Combination

One of the most important methods used during meditation is the combination of the letters of a word or a divine name or, alternatively, a set of words or names. The origin of this method is found in the Sepher Yetsira, the Book of Formation.

The 22 letters of the alphabet are divided into three categories:

Three main or mother letters;
Seven double letters;
Twelve simple letters.
"The 22 letters, He traced them, carved them, multiplied them, weighed them, and permuted them, and with them He formed all creatures and everything that was created. And how did He multiply them?

Aleph with all All with Aleph Bet with all All with Bet. Gimel with all All with Gimel...

All were spinning in a circle: thus resulting in two hundred and thirty-one gates. All words came from the same name."

If each letter is combined with all the others, this results in 22 letters multiplied by 22 = 484. Subtract 22 combinations where the two letters are identical (aleph-aleph, bet-bet), which gives 462. In these 462 combinations, half is a repetition of combinations that already exist: for example, aleph-bet and bet-aleph.

Thus, there remain 231 truly original combinations. Some comments explain the name Israel in this way: Israel reads yech raal, meaning "there are 231." The name of Israel would be linked to the combination of the letters.

Another Mishnah from the Sepher Yetsira teaches:

"The 12 simple letters, with the others, the Creator invented, traced, multiplied, opposed, inverted. And what is the way to permute them and multiply them?

Two stones (letters) build two houses (words) Three stones build six houses (words) Four stones, twenty houses Five stones, one hundred and twenty houses Seven stones, five thousand and forty houses And after this, you can count until you reach what the mouth cannot say, nor the ear hear..."

(Sepher Yetsira, III, 4.) Thirty-two years to reach a billion. The total number of combinations far exceeds the duration of a lifetime...

The modalities of combinations are varied. Some consider only the divine names, introducing variations due to vowels. Others focus on the names of the organs of the body or on the letters associated with the organs of the body, as explicitly stated in the Sepher Yetsira. We will return to this subject.

The Tsérouf, or combinatorial art, provokes, with the help of methodical meditation, new states of consciousness. Abulafia, who worked extensively with this method, compared it to music.

CHAPTER XVI

Meditation and Music

The systematic practice of meditation, as taught by Rabbi Abraham Abulafia, truly evokes a sensation very close to the one felt when listening to musical harmonies. The science of combination is a music of pure thought, in which the alphabet takes the place of the musical scale. The entire system shows a close similarity to musical principles applied not to sounds, but to thought in meditation. We experience compositions and modifications of motifs and combinations of all possible varieties.

In his book Gan Naoul (The Closed Garden), Abulafia explains, in an important passage, the parallel between the influence exerted by music and the technique of combining letters.

"Know that the method of Tsérouf [combination of letters] can be compared to music; for the ear listens to sounds of diverse combinations, according to the character of the melody and the instrument. Thus, two different string instruments, the lute and the harp [kinnor and névèl], combine their sounds, and the ear perceives their variations and harmonies, experiencing, in fact, a sensation identical to that of the 'languishes of love.'

From the ear, the sensation travels to the heart, and from the heart to the spleen. Joy is renewed by the union of different tones that seek always new pleasure. It is impossible to produce such pleasure except through the combination of sounds, and the same rule holds true for the combination of letters.

Let the first string be played – comparable to the first letter aleph – then the second, corresponding to bet, and so on... The various sounds combine, and the mysteries of these combinations cheer the heart through the ear.

Thus, proceed with the method that consists of permuting the external letters with a pen, according to the following combination:

aleph-mem-chin mem-aleph-chin mem-chin-aleph chin-aleph-mem chin-mem-aleph aleph-chin-mem

and so on...”

There is an effect of music and the combinations of letters on the body that is comparable to a musical instrument.

“For just as the owner of a garden has the power to water it at will with the water from the streams, so the musician has the power to water his limbs with his soul, and thanks to the great Name, blessed be He; such is the meaning of the verse: 'And while the musician played his instrument, the divine breath took hold of him' (2 Kings 3:15). Such is the meaning of the kinnor that was fixed under David's bed and which he himself played in the verse: 'Praise Him with the lute and the harp' (Psalm 150:3). However, this would not be possible except after receiving the divine influx, called the sixty-two letters, and the knowledge of their ways.”

“The body, like the garden, is the master of vegetation. And the soul is Eden, the master of all delights, where the body is planted. And the hidden meaning of gan Eden (the Garden of Eden) is 'ad naguèn (the permutation of the letters themselves) [which means: until he touches], for prophecy appears when the servant sings, as it is written: 'And while the musician played, the prophecy took hold of him [the prophet Elisha]' (2 Kings 3:15).”

The prophetic experience passes through the music of the permutations of letters; we draw attention to this very important permutation: the expression gan Eden (Garden of Eden) has the same letters as 'ad naguèn, meaning “until he touches.”

168

In the context of meditation, the music of the letters opens the paths of prophecy.

"The directed activity of the adept who engages in combining and separating the letters in his meditation, thus composing motifs with separate groups, combining them one with another, and superimposing their combinations in all directions, is for Abulafia no more meaningless or incomprehensible than the activity of the composer. Just as the musician expresses in sounds without words 'the world in a new way' – to quote Schopenhauer – and ascends to heights and descends to depths without end, so also occurs with the mystic: for him, the closed doors of the soul open in the music of pure thought that is no longer linked to the 'senses,' and in the ecstasy of the deepest harmonies that have their origin in the movement of the letters of the great Name, these doors open wide on the path that leads to God."

In the meditative practice proposed by Abulafia, each letter represents an entire world for the mystic who surrenders to its contemplation.

However, as an essential observation, any language, and not just the Hebrew language, is transformed into a transcendental intermediary.

CHAPTER XVII

The Five Modalities of Being

In the texts of the Bible, and later in the Midrash and Kabbalah, there are five expressions used to designate the soul.

By "soul," we understand that which allows a person to have a harmonious life on the physical, psychic, and spiritual planes.

These five expressions are:

Néfèch
Rouah
Nechama
Hayya
Yehida
All these terms are found in biblical texts and can take on meanings with multiple nuances. The meaning we will give to them is more appropriate for the meditation exercises we will propose and does not exclude other, more sophisticated interpretations.

Some commentators see these expressions as five hierarchically organized levels, with néfèch being the lowest and yehida the highest. It seems more accurate to speak of the different modalities of the human being, which enable the proper functioning of the human structure.

Néfèch

From a semantic point of view, the word néfèch means, at
the same time, in its verbal form "to rest, to relax," and "to
animate, to reanimate." The form hitpaèl, hitnafèch, means "to
breathe strongly." In its substantive form, néfèch means "soul,
life, breath," and also, in a common sense, "person, living
being." It also has meanings such as "will, desire," "feeling,
passion," "chest, throat," and even "memorial monument."

The néfèch is the living being that can rest after an effort,
as it is in a dialectical and alternating movement of "work-
rest," "tension-relaxation," an alternation that allows it to rest
and "breathe" so that the effort does not lead to the ultimate
consequence: death. Néfèch: a living being that breathes.
However, it does not act here through the breath but through
the movement of life in the body's infrastructure—organs
and cells—which, together, form a space of incessant change,
taking in the substances necessary for its energy to function
and expelling the substances and waste that oppose the vital
force of proper functioning.

One of the biblical references presents this definition: ki néfèch
k'ol bassar damo hi, meaning: "For the néfèch of all flesh is
its blood." And Rashi specifies in his commentary, to leave no
doubt: hanèfèch hi hadam — "The néfèch is the blood." The
word dam means blood, which literally constitutes one-third
of a man; hence the name Adam (aleph-dalèt-mèm).

The néfèch, as blood, is what enables cellular and organic
respiration. It is the circulation of vital substances that
energize the entire human body in its most physical
dimension. The other meanings of néfèch are analogical and
metaphorical. In this way, will, desire, feeling, and passion
are modalities of a being in which the body is physiologically
well energized. Blood not only distributes oxygen but also the
entire set of vital substances assimilated by food, which pass
into the blood during digestion.

Thus, thanks to the blood, different cells of different organs receive oxygen, water, proteins, fats, and salts, and can live, grow, and reproduce. Cellular waste is thus removed and eliminated via the blood before being filtered by the kidneys and other organs.

Rouah

The word rouah means "wind, air, breath, spirit." It is the action of a part of the respiratory system, from the mouth and nose to the lungs. Regarding oxygen, the lungs are the "interface" between the inside and outside. The circulation of air between the nose and mouth on one hand and the lungs on the other is rouah.

This term underwent two evolutions. Initially, it meant "spirit," and later "word." In fact, speech is also a modulation of air over the vocal cords. In the Zohar and Tiqouné Zohar, the organs of rouah are found in the Tetragrammaton under the form of the letters vav (the trachea) and the two hé (the lungs). We will return to address the relationship between letters and the body later.

The physiology of breathing, although very complex, can be schematically presented as a place of change at the level of the lungs, which assimilate the oxygen passing through the blood, carried by red blood cells, and release the carbon dioxide carried by the blood from the cells and carried by hemoglobin. When we breathe, we usually think "air-oxygen" (in and out), forgetting the articulation between the circulatory and respiratory systems.

Nechama

Interestingly, this term, more than the previous two, became synonymous with "soul" in the vague and popular sense of the word. In fact, originally, nechama comes from the root nacham, which means "to breathe." The word néchèm or nechima refers to breathing, the breath.

172

Thus, it is difficult to make a distinction between rouah and nechama. However, nechama can be explained as the different modalities of breathing, inspiration-expiration. Rouah maintains the earlier meaning related to the physiology of gaseous changes in the lungs.

Haya

This term also appears in the Book of Genesis when man is formed and is associated with the words néfèch and nechama: vayitseré hachem Elohim ét haadam afar min haadama, vayipah nichmat hayyim, vaychi haadam lenéfèch haya, which means: "And YHVH-ELOHIM formed man from the dust of the ground. He breathed into his nostrils the breath of life (nichmat hayyim), and man became a living being (néfèch haya)."

The word haya, from the verb hayo, means "to live." Hayyim is life. According to the biblical text, néfèch haya designates all living creatures, human or animal. It is assumed that haya represents the circulation of energy that passes through the body. Haya is the vital in the sense of "energy."

Yehida

Yehida is the highest level. Etymologically, this word means "singularity," "oneness." In an initial, physical analysis, it corresponds to the unique way of being of each individual, undoubtedly tied to "genetic identity." It is, in fact, a mode of being at the ethical level that corresponds to the unique in each person, from which the idea of responsibility comes.

For the Hebrew tradition, each human being has a unique and singular vocation that only they can fulfill. They must respond to this vocation, this unique project. This is their responsibility.

CHAPTER XVIII
Body and Script

According to the Sefer Yetzirah (Book of Formation), there is a relationship between the letters of the alphabet and the organs and parts of the body. The Tiqquné Zohar, a book of themes and variations on the first word of the Bible, Bereishit, also emphasizes this analogy of "body and script."

The modalities of these relationships are complex. Sometimes they are direct, other times associative—whether through homophony or homomorphy—or even through structural-word adequacy.

For example, the word for "hand" in Hebrew is yad: yod-dalet, two letters whose semantic energy equals 14 [yod = 10; dalet = 4].

Furthermore, anatomically, the hand consists of fourteen phalanges!

The relationship between numerals and letters is rarely so evident. One aspect of meditation is to build these body-letter connections. Here, reference will be made to the teachings of the Sefer Yetzirah, where it consistently insists on the Hebrew word for a given organ or member, a word whose knowledge is crucial for being put into practice in meditation techniques.

Postures and Letters

At first glance, postures are the mimicry of the form of the letters. They may be unique or multiple, depending on the complexity of the letter. Hebrew meditation does not definitively codify the body positions corresponding to the letters, leaving the freedom for each participant to invent their own choreography.

However, regarding the three basic forms—point-line-plane—corresponding to yod-vav-dalet, the following guidelines can be given:

Any posture of self-bending, twisting, coiling, fetalization, etc., will represent the letter yod;

Any posture where the body expresses a vertical line will represent the letter vav;
Any posture where the body forms a right angle will represent the letter dalet...
Some yoga postures and other techniques will suitably allow for the proper expression of these three fundamental letters. The letters can also be written on the ground. For example, the letter dalet can be formed by two people lying on the ground in such a way that they form a right angle.
Some letters can only be written in pairs. This is the case for hé and qof.
At the end of this book, all the letters will be described to facilitate these postures.

CHAPTER XIX
The Points in Vibration: The Vowels

After studying the structure of the Hebrew letters, which are all consonants and, therefore, purely of the visible and mentally legible order, it is necessary to learn about the vowels that will form the basis of respiration.
The ten Hebrew vowels are formed by points, except in three cases where a line is involved.
We will proceed in order: from the point to the points and the line. There are three vowels that are composed of a single point. It is the placement of the point in relation to the letter that gives it its meaning, and in a certain way, also its significance. The higher the point, the more valued the letter that bears it, and the more semantic energy it carries.
The position in relation to the letter can even be more important than the number of points that make up the vowel.
The first vowel, in order of importance, is the holam: it is a point that sits at the top left of the letter and gives the sound "o."
We will provide all examples with the letter aleph.

Most often, the holam is carried by the letter vav and is called holam-vav.

When pronounced, only two letters use the holam: the first letter, yod, and the 19th letter, qof, whose numerical values are 10 and 100, respectively.

The holam is the soul of the yod, it gives it its existence in language, in the world of meanings. Rabbi Yossef Gikatilla explains in Le Jardin des noyers: the 10 is "holy" and the holam, which sets it in motion, is the "holy of holies."

We find the holam point in everything related to the tens: in 10, in 100 (a ten of tens). As for its shape, it resembles the letter yod and has an initial numerical value of 10. But this is not pertinent, because it would imply that the holam carries the same semantic weight as the chourouq, for example, which is also made up of a point, but located not above the letter, but in its center.

The numerical value of the holam is that of the word holam: hèt-lamèd-mèm = 78, which has the same semantic weight as the word hasdo (Divine Generosity): hèt-samèkh-dalèt-vav = 08 + 60 + 04 + 06 = 78, and it also has the numerical value of the Tetragrammaton: yod-hé-vav-hé = 10 + 05 + 06 + 05 = 26 (3 x 26 = 78).

What is also important is the name of this vowel: holam, which means dream. It opens the doors of the dream. The combination of the three letters of the root should make us reflect on salt: mélah (mèm-lamèd-hèt), bread: léhem (lamèd-hèt-mèm), dance: mahol, disease, and forgiveness: mahala, mohel.

This set of semantic context unfolds in the attempt to find all combinations that involve the three letters of the root: this is the method called tsérouf.

The examples we will provide will clearly demonstrate a form of approach that could be applied to all the vowels.

The second vowel is the chourouq. It is also formed by a point, but it is placed in the center, to the left of the letter. The example with aleph is as follows:

The third vowel is the hiriq: a point below the letter.

 hiriq

Holam, Chourouq, and Hiriq form the first group of vowels, those that consist of a single point. The second group consists of vowels made up of two points. This group includes tséré, which is pronounced "é", and chéva (the silent "e").

chéva   *tséré*

The third group: the vowels made up of three points, including ségol (é) and qoubouts (ou).

ségol   *qoubouts*

The fourth group includes two vowels composed of a line, either alone or associated with a point. This is the series of "a": patah and qamats.

The qamats, and this is not always clear, is formed by a line and a point.

The fifth group consists of mixed vowels, which are formed by the combination of two already existing vowels. Rabbi Moché Cordovéro focuses in his commentary on the Yetsira solely on the chéva-qamats: the combination of a chéva and a qamats.

The name of each vowel has a specific meaning. For example:

Holam: the dimension of the dream.
Chourouq: the sibilance and everything related to it.
Hiriq: to rub, grind the teeth.
Tséré: narrowing, closure, difficulty, retention.
Chéva: that which is void, the useless.
Ségol: violet (the color), a community, adaptation, treasure, precious.
Patah: the door, the opening.
Qamats: hand that closes.
The semantic weight of the vowels is not based on their form but according to the name, unfolded in a consonantal manner:

Holam: hèt-lamèd-mèm = 8 + 30 + 40 = 78.
Chourouq: chin-rèch-qof = 300 + 200 + 100 = 600.
Hiriq: hèt-rèch-qof = 8 + 200 + 100 = 308.
Tséré: tsadé-rèch-yod = 90 + 200 + 10 = 300.
Chéva (two possible forms):
Chin-vav-aleph = 300 + 6 + 1 = 307.
Chin-bèt-aleph = 300 + 2 + 1 = 303.
Ségol: samèkh-guimel-lamèd = 60 + 3 + 30 = 93.
Patah: pé-tav-hét = 80 + 400 + 8 = 488.

Qamats: quof-mèm-tsadé = 100 + 40 + 90 = 230.
The existence of different vowels doesn't only produce sounds and differentiated meanings but also allows for a variety of vibrations that have important effects on the human organism. The emission of vowels during exhalation causes a self-massage vibration in the organs, making the vibrations reach the deeper tissues and nerve cells. Blood circulation intensifies in the tissues and organs involved. Internal secretion glands, which release their hormones directly into the blood and lymph, are stimulated (pituitary, pineal, thyroid, thymus, adrenal glands, gonads).

The sympathetic and vagus nerves are not exempt from the beneficial influence of vocal vibrations. The respiratory system's muscles are sometimes relaxed and strengthened. Breathing expands, and with it, the oxygen supply to the entire body. Electromagnetic waves are also emitted by these vibrations, spreading throughout the body and adding dynamism and joy to life. Concentration improves. The whole body relaxes under the effect of an internal vibro-massage that, psychologically, releases inhibitions... harmonizing the entire psyche.

In the next chapters, we will explore the application of these vibrational considerations. Furthermore, the function of the ear is not only in its ability to understand information, messages, and other auditory signs. Perhaps it is also, and primarily, the main generator of nerve energy. It behaves like a dynamo, and most of the energy the brain needs comes precisely from the dynamogenic action of the auditory system... The ear ensures cortical load; it is a generator of energy. It has a dynamizing power.

Among the effects related to energization, we can define those linked to charging sounds and those corresponding to discharge sounds. Low-frequency sounds are more easily integrated into discharge zones. High-frequency sounds are true energy generators.

Chapter XX
The Practice of Meditation
Breathing: Energizing the Letters

The first moment of breathing allows for the awareness of the articulation of the three dimensions: Néfèch, Rouah, Nechama, which we previously presented in the chapter titled The Five Modalities of Being.

We highlight the fundamental idea regarding breathing: the true organ of breathing is the blood. The lungs are merely the place where it happens.

"For it is precisely the blood that actively takes hold of the oxygen from the air, with which it comes into contact through the lung sponge. It is exactly the blood that releases the excess CO_2. It also acts on the respiratory centers in the brainstem, triggering the movements of the chest cavity and diaphragm according to their needs, which represent the needs of the entire organism. In other words, the lungs are, first and foremost, a sponge full of blood, a double-faced sponge capable of inhaling the outside air. It is the blood that enables cellular respiration. The blood — it is important to realize this — is much more than a simple physiological liquid, whose color is due to the presence of red blood cells. The blood is, in the strictest sense, a fluid organ, a living organ, and one of the largest in the body, as it 'occupies' five to six liters! Except for the skin, no organ has this kind of ponderous importance!"

As the diaphragm compresses and the chest opens, the lung sponge fills with blood seeking contact with the air. The exercise, which we will soon begin, is based on this awareness.

Although theoretically it can be practiced in any position, for our learning, we will choose the position lying on the floor, on the back. In fact, one can adopt the usual relaxation position: the feet are slightly apart, arms resting at the sides of the body without touching, with the palms of the hands preferably facing upwards.

The exercise begins by focusing on the air entering the lungs and the relationship with the blood flow from the entire body, triggered by the expansion of the chest. Initially, the process is done analytically. One performs a slow and complete inhalation, imagining that blood is being drawn from outside the legs into the chest, through each toe, flowing into the lungs.

In the exhalation, one imagines the chest compressing the lung sponge and sending purified and enriched blood back to the legs, down to the toes. A new inhalation follows, imagining that blood is being drawn from the abdominal organs into the thoracic area. In the following exhalation, one imagines sending it back, well-oxygenated and full of vitality. The next inhalation focuses on the hands, fingers, and arms. Finally — and this is no less important — during a deep inhalation, one perceives (as it is literally perceptible) that blood is drawn from outside the brain and returned there during the exhalation.

Physiologically, the brain changes volume during the respiratory process. Now, during the next inhalation, imagine that the blood is drained from the entire body into the chest, and during the exhalation, send it back to the entire organism as the chest contracts.

In Hebrew meditation, the technique of breathing we just mentioned is practiced in a second phase, consciously and intentionally overlaying the Hebrew name that will be mentally visualized over the organ or member.

Thus, it is not only the body, in its materiality, that is energized, but also the letters that underlie it. For example, in the case of the left foot, the word Réguèl (rèch-guimel-lamèd) is mentally visualized. Inhalation involves imagining the extraction of blood from the foot, as well as vital energy (haya) from the word Réguèl.

In exhalation, the attention should be directed to the return of energy to the three letters rèch-guimel-lamèd.

This exercise has many variants. It can be made more complex by dedicating one breath to each letter, specifying mentally whether it is the right or left side (in Hebrew, yamin and smol). It all depends on the time available for these meditations. Some people do not visualize the "word" for the foot but rather the letter assigned to it by the Sepher Yetsira, as we previously explained. For example, the letter tsadé for the right foot and the letter qof for the left foot.

In addition to the sensation of warmth that one feels in each part of the body intentionally meditated, one must focus on the energetic aspect of this process.

As we emphasized, through many repetitions, the energy that travels and circulates in the body uses language as a support. A statically bodily language will have a body that is tendentially static, and vice versa. The essential goal of meditation is to produce a language in motion for a being in motion.

Breathing and Vibration

According to Rabbi Abraham Abulafia, meditative breathing consists of three parts:

Inspiration
Retention of air in the lungs
Expiration
As Mosche Idel observes in his book about Abulafia, this is the "triadic" breathing of yoga. In Abulafia, as in yoga, the exhalation should last roughly twice as long as the inhalation.

The exhalation is performed after the retention of the air and is accompanied by the emission of a vowel sound, which aims to control the flow and regularity of the air and produce various vibrations, as we explained in Chapter XIX.

Just as in Portuguese, there are five basic vowels and five nuances of sound.

In Abulafia's technique, only five vowels are used: holam [O], qamats [A], hiriq [I], tséré [é], and qoubouts [ou].

The First Exercise

It consists of performing five "triadic" breaths, emitting a different sound with each slow exhalation after retention: A, E, I, O, U.

"From a therapeutic perspective, this combination of air and sounds produces specific vibrations that promote better circulation of blood and vital energy, and positively affect the nervous system. Each sound has its own field of action:

A (holam) acts on the chest center and diaphragm, toning the heart.
E (qamats) acts on the esophagus, the three upper ribs, and the upper lung lobes.
I (tséré) acts on the throat, vocal cords, larynx, and thyroid.
O (hiriq) vibrates upwards to the larynx, nose, forehead, and dissipates headaches.
U (qoubouts) acts on all the abdominal organs, such as the stomach, liver, intestines, and gonads.
Once in a comfortable position, one must focus on the "emotion" that the vowel awakens. Then, inhale through the nose, hold the breath, and exhale slowly while humming the vocal sound, concentrating on the area where the vibration is located, emptying the lungs as slowly and deeply as possible, but without excessive effort.

This vibratory massage circulates accumulated tensions in the tissues, which are then eliminated, while the well-oxygenated blood flow nourishes and revitalizes the cells."

The Second Exercise

This will activate the same process, but adding consonantal variations to the vowel modulations. Thus, there will be 22 dyads, each combining the letter aleph with another letter from the alphabet. These dyads will be modulated according to the table below, which serves as a guide. The table associates the letters aleph and yod in fifty different combinations.

Therefore, with 5 vowels and 22 letters combined with aleph, there are 1,100 possible combinations.

אָ	אֲ	אָ	אַ	אָ	אֶ	אָ
אַ	אַ	אָ	אָ	אַ	אָ	אַ
אָ	אֶ	אֶ	אָ	אֶ	אָ	אֶ
אָ	אָ	אָ	אָ	אָ	אָ	אָ
אָ	אָ	אָ	אָ	אָ	אָ	אָ
אָ	אָ	אָ	אָ	אָ	אָ	אָ

The Third Exercise

This consists of visualizing the letters that are pronounced and moving the head in a motion that describes the shape of the letter. This movement can accompany a real vocal emission or a mental and silent internalization of the letter's sound. The shape of the letter will be discussed in the next chapter.

Visualization and Writing

After the exercises related to the "circulatory breath" and the energizing of the body-letters and "vibratory vowels," Hebrew meditation dedicates itself to a set of visualizations.

According to the technique proposed by Abulafia, the aim is to use the shapes of the Hebrew letters as a support for meditation. "In calm and semi-clarity, take a fountain pen and a board." Adapted to modern materials, it is enough to use a white sheet of paper (without lines), black ink, and a writing instrument that can make both thick and fine strokes (a pen cut at an angle).

First Exercise:

After a session of breathing and vocalization (no more than ten minutes each), draw a complete series of letters from the Hebrew alphabet according to the ritual form proposed at the end of this paragraph. The goal here is not simply to perform a writing technique exercise, but to internalize these forms, and then to understand what impact they have on us.

In the first phase, you must let yourself intuitively absorb these forms.

In the second phase, take each letter one by one and meditate, visualizing with closed eyes everything that each letter evokes on both an individual and collective level. You need to place yourself, literally, in the mental state of aleph, bèt, etc.

This exercise can be done alone or in a group. In the first case, after the meditation, write down all of the associations in a notebook that will be dedicated for this purpose. When done in a group, the personal meditation is followed by a collective discussion on the meaning and evocation of each letter.

It is important to emphasize that everything that can be said here is merely a personal interpretation, not a dogmatic truth to be imposed: a proposition, not an imposition.

After this collective discussion, each person will return to their notebook to write down the main points or details from the session.

The goal is to learn the dynamic of how the letters are formed and to be able to later visualize them from memory.

Second Exercise:

This consists of meditating on the letters of your Hebrew first name. Follow the same procedure as before.

First phase: Write down the letters until you visually memorize them.
Second phase: Look for all the associations that these letters evoke, write them down, and discuss them in a dialogue with another person.

In this exercise, you will use Tsérouf, the combination of letters, which means you will try to write as many words as possible using the letters from your first name.

For people who do not have a Hebrew first name, they should choose one and verify its exact spelling in Hebrew.

The third phase consists of returning to the breathing exercises, in which the sounds emitted will be the vowels and consonants (first just the vowels, and then the vowels combined with the consonants) of the first name.

Example: Abraham
In vowels: A – A – A
In vowels-consonants: AB – RA – HAM

Third Exercise:

This is an extension of the previous one. It aims to do the same work with the first names of your parents, grandparents, etc. The objective of this work is to inscribe oneself in a living temporality that encompasses both the past and the future.

For the Hebrew tradition, there is no future without the past.

The fourth exercise logically follows this one. It consists of a meditation on the first names of your children or on the first names you would like to give them.

All these meditations involve reflection, visualization, writing, breathing, and the movement of the head or the entire body "dancing" the shape of the letters. In this way, a name becomes a chain of movements.

This work should be done slowly and regularly. There is no need to dedicate more than two hours per day to it.

Thus, in each session, focus on a single letter (and a single vowel) when you first discover it. In subsequent sessions, begin with a new letter, and then integrate the conclusions from previous sessions.

Fundamental Observation

These exercises on names are only preliminary to the work on the Divine Names, which is much too complex to be exposed in this small introduction. However, we have provided sufficient information in previous chapters to begin an interesting meditation.

You can dedicate numerous sessions to the Tetragrammaton YHVH by applying all the breathing exercises described. However, it is essential to dissociate the mental visualization from the vocalization in these meditations. Since the Tetragrammaton is unpronounceable, it cannot be vocalized.

In these exercises, the focus is only on the consonants, which will be visualized in a dynamic way. We have previously explained the graphic structure of the Tetragrammaton, based on the combination of three elements: point-line-plane.

Here, the aim is to follow the path from nothingness to the inscription of the Tetragrammaton and from the Tetragrammaton back to nothingness. The process is as follows:

You must visualize nothingness with the help of a

representation of whiteness, from which the point (yod) will suddenly emerge, then the line (vav), and finally the plane (dalèt). After this, mentally write the Tetragrammaton, following the evolution of its graphic structure.

In the second phase, do the reverse process to return to nothingness.

This exercise corresponds to the dialectic of the "I" and "nothing," as explained in Chapter IV.

This set of preliminary exercises, which do not require any knowledge beyond that of the Hebrew alphabet, is but a drop in the infinite sea of Hebrew texts and represents only a few pages among the tens of thousands of pages in the texts of Jewish mysticism. To give a small idea, the current edition of the Zohar consists of two dozen volumes, each with over three hundred pages. One must add to that the monumental work of Rabbi Abraham Abulafia (about ten treatises), the work of Rabbi Moshe Cordovero, and the fundamental work of Rabbi Isaac Luria (two dozen important volumes). Not to mention, of course, the Talmud, the Midrash, etc.

One cannot practice Hebrew meditation without accompanying it with sessions of study of the texts from the tradition. Only this parallel study ensures that the meditative technique does not dry up.

CHAPTER XXI
Description of the Letters

Clear and recognizable writing: The scribe should focus on forming letters that are clear and easily recognizable, always prioritizing the beauty of their writing. Minor modifications do not disqualify the work as long as the silhouette of the letter is respected.

Differences between Sephardic and Ashkenazi traditions: There are subtle differences between Sephardic (Spanish) and Ashkenazi (German) writing styles. The first is called Ktav Vallich, while the second is known as Ktav Beit Yosseph. According to a widely accepted opinion, one can occasionally adopt the writing style of a different community, which allows some flexibility in practice.

Unity of the letters: Each letter must be formed as a single piece, except for the hé and qof, whose left leg is separated from the rest of the letter. If there is any break in the letters or if two parts touch in a place where they should be separate, the letter will be disqualified.

Taguim on the letters: The letters guimèl, zayin, tèt, noun (and final noun), 'ayin, tsadé (and final tsadé), and chin have their left heads adorned with three small lines. These lines are called tag (in plural, taguim). These taguim are very thin, well-spaced from each other, and should touch the head of the letter. They consist of a fine leg, covered with a small hat.

ALEPH

The upper limb [1] resembles a yod slightly tilted to the right, crowned with a small stroke [2]. This yod is, by necessity, connected by its "leg" [3] to the central element of the aleph, ideally at its midpoint. This central element is slightly inclined upwards at its lower end [4]. The lower limb [5] resembles a yod connected to the central element by a stroke [6] that deviates (according to the teachings of Rabbi Ari Za'l, its shape is preferably that of a small "inverted dalèt").

In the Ktav Vallich script, the upper limb is not exactly like a yod; its leg exits from the right side, closer to the end, and connects to the central element a bit lower than its midpoint. As for the lower limb, it has a small leg turned to the left.

BÈT

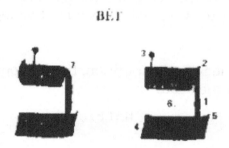

Care must be taken to ensure that its sides [1] form true right angles, in order to distinguish it from the kaf. The bèt is typically adorned with two small strokes: one over the upper angle [2], directed toward the aleph, and the second near the "face" of the letter [3]. The pedestal [4] extends to the right and ends with a small protrusion [5]. The height and width of the bèt are equal to three thicknesses of the quill (the unit of measurement for writing = the thickness of the stroke produced when the quill is laid flat), and the height of its inner space [6] will be the value of one quill thickness.

In the Sefardic script, the upper angle [7] is often rounded, and the small stroke mentioned earlier is not added.

GUIMÈL

The "head" [1] is thick, the right leg [2] is thin and extends a little further down than the lower left member [3]. The latter extends and rises slightly towards the dalèt. The leg connects to the center [4] of the head, and the head is crowned by three strokes [5]. The junction [6] between the two legs is not very thick.

According to the Sefardic tradition, the leg connects to the right end [7] of the head.

DALÈT

 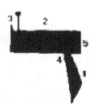

The leg [1] is slightly shorter than the "roof" [2], so as not to resemble a final kaf. The leg descends slightly inclined to the right. In the dalèt, a small stroke [3] is added near the left end of the roof. The angle is quite tight (almost square) [4], to differentiate the dalèt from the rèch, and it is even preferable to add a thick stroke to its upper part [5] to accentuate this difference.

In the Sefardic script, the leg is almost always vertical.

HÉ

The roof of the hé will be adorned with a small stroke [1] near its left end, and the angle [2] will be square, as in the dalèt (and not rounded as in the rèch). The distance separating the left leg [3] will not exceed the thickness of a pen, but it should be placed in such a way that the free space is clearly noticeable when reading the Torah. If the left leg touches the roof, even slightly, the hé will be disqualified for reading. This left leg should also have a thickness proportional to its height; as for its shape, it resembles an inverted yod. The right leg [4] is identical to the one in the dalèt.

According to the Sefardic custom, the left leg can be a simple vertical stroke.

Note: According to the teachings of Rabbi Ari Za'l, the hé in the Divine Name has a slightly different form.

VAV

Its head [1] should be very short to ensure that the vav does not resemble a rèch, and its leg [2] should be quite long to avoid resembling a yod. It is recommended that the angle [3] be rounded, and that the leg tapers as it descends.

Its leg [1] should not be too long, in order to avoid resembling a final noun. In case of doubt, the letter should be recognized by a child. Its head [2] will extend laterally so that it surpasses both sides of the leg; its shape will be that of a square with three small strokes placed above it.

In Sefardic script, the head of the zayin most often appears as a diamond shape, slightly tilted upwards.

HÈT

It is usually formed by two zayins, connected at the top by a kind of pointed hat [1]. The right head is rounded on its right side [2], while the left head is topped with a small stroke [3]. The space [4] between them should be, at most, the thickness of a pen. If the hèt is written without the "hat," but with a flat roof [5], it is still valid, even if the roof is quite long.

The right head will curve onto itself [1], rounding out. The leg that extends from it will also be rounded [2] at the bottom. The left side of the letter consists of a vertical leg [3] attached to the pedestal at a right angle, and a square head topped with three small strokes.

YOD

It should feature, on the right, a leg [1] slightly inclined to the left. Its left side [2] is adorned with two small strokes: the upper one [3] is longer than the lower one [4], and both must be shorter than the leg. The absence of either of these lower elements (and perhaps even the small upper stroke) makes the letter unsuitable for reading. The body of the yod resembles a square [5] that is firmly set, with the right side [6] rounded, and it is carved with the thickness of a pen. The proportions of the yod must be strictly adhered to, as any change risks making it look like a vav, rèch, hèt, or lamèd.

According to the Sephardic custom, the head of the yod is most often slightly inclined [7] to the right. Its left half rises and contracts, eventually forming a small stroke [8]. Some authorities state that the yod is not disqualified by the absence of the small lower left stroke.

KAF

To better differentiate it from the bèt, it will be rounded at the top [1] and at the bottom [2]. The central space should have at least the height of one pen thickness, and the edges will be vertically aligned [3]. It is important to avoid writing it too narrow, as this would make it resemble a noun.

KAF FINAL.

Its shape should be such that, if it were curved, it would turn into a kaf. Therefore, the length of its top should be half the length of its leg, and its corner [1] must be rounded. If the top is elongated to the point of making it resemble a rèch, and if the corner forms a right angle, it will be necessary to correct the letter by adding ink to round it off.

According to the Sephardic tradition, a final kaf written with a right angle can be validated.

LAMÈD

Its shape is that of a kaf overlain by a vav. In general, the base [1] of this kaf is written shorter than its upper part [2]. The junction with the vav forms a right angle [3] at the end of the kaf. The head of the vav is adorned with two small strokes [4]: the one on the right is slightly longer than the one on the left.

According to Sephardic custom, the body of the lamèd is not like a kaf; it is initially like a rèch with a short leg [5], and then continues with a diagonal line [6] to the left, which curves slightly towards the base [7] at its end.

MÈM

Its shape is roughly that of a vav joined to a kaf; however, its lower corner [1] will be at an angle, not rounded. Its roof is flat [2] and extends up to the vertical [3] of its pedestal. The vav is slightly inclined; care must be taken to ensure it does not touch the pedestal [4].

In Sephardic writing, the roof is rounded [5] and does not extend [6] to the edge of its pedestal.

It is written with a slightly rounded top on the right [1], but its other corners [2] will be at right angles. Its roof extends beyond the left side [3] by about the thickness of a pen. Some also form the upper right corner with an angle.

NOUN

Its head is the same as that of the zayin, square in shape and topped by three small strokes. The neck releases [1] from the center of the head, and tilts downward to the right, before connecting [2] to the rounded pedestal. The latter extends to the left, surpassing [3] the limit of its head. According to the Sephardic tradition, the leg of the noun releases from the right end [4] of the head.

NOUN FINAL

Its shape is that of the zayin, but more elongated, with its cut being about five pen thicknesses. In case of confusion between these two letters, it should be made identifiable by a child. In the final noun, the leg must, without exception, start from the middle [1] of the head, and not from the right end (which would give it the shape of an elongated vav). Here too, the head is adorned with three small strokes.

SAMEKH

The top will be flat [1], and the base narrow [2]. The two lower corners [3] and the upper right corner [4] will be rounded, while the upper left corner [5] will form a right angle. The "top" extends slightly beyond the letter. According to the Sephardic tradition, the left leg [6] does not form a regular curve, but rather breaks [7] and leans to the right.

'AYIN

The right head is slightly tilted [1] upwards; its leg initially stands almost vertically [2], slightly leaning to the left, and its lower part is slanted to the left [3], forming a pedestal that thickens. The left part of the 'ayin has exactly the shape of a zayin and connects [4] at the start of the pedestal. Some give the left head the form of a vav with a square head, also adorned with three small strokes.

PÉ

Its upper right corner [1] will form a right angle. As for the lower right corner [2], it will be rounded on the outside. Its upper left extremity is overlaid with a small stroke [3], which extends downward and widens to the right [4] within the foot, forming an inverted vav. This vav should not touch the body of the foot at any point other than the leg it is connected to. The central space [5] of the foot has the shape of a bèt.

In the Sephardic script, the base of the vav is usually adorned with a small lateral stroke.

PÉ FINAL

Its upper right corner [1] must form a right angle. Its leg should be long enough to be curved, giving the letter the shape of a final foot. Some round the upper right angle.

TSADÉ

Its general shape is that of a noun from which a slightly inclined yod is attached. The leg of the yod connects at the middle of the height [1] of the noun, not at its lower half, to avoid resembling an 'ayin. The neck of the noun connects [2] to the head at its middle, not at its end. This head is adorned with three small strokes. The lower right corner [3] is rounded. The base extends to the left [4] at least until the vertical line of the left head.

According to the Sephardic custom (and also according to the tradition attributed to Rabbi Ari Za'l), the two heads of the tsadé [1] are two yods, with the one on the right being inverted.

TSADÉ FINAL

Its two heads [1] are the same as those of the tsadé, but its leg [2] descends straight, long enough to give the letter the shape of the final tsadé.

QOF

Its roof is adorned with a small vertical stroke [1] on the left. Its right leg should be distinctly bent [2] towards its left leg. The latter [3] will not touch either the roof or the right leg, staying about half a pen thickness [4] away from the roof, and will descend, slightly tilting to the right. The shape of this leg is that of a final noun, and it hangs under the left end of the roof.

In the Sephardic script, the right leg is not truly curved, but splits into two segments: the first [6], thinner, directs to the left. As for the left leg, it is thin at both ends and thickens in the middle.

Its corner [1] is quite rounded. Its leg is slightly shorter than its roof, distinguishing it from the final kaf. Its roof is long enough to differentiate it from the vav.

CHIN

Its three components, from right to left, are shaped like a vav [1], yod [2], and zayin [3]. The zayin stands upright and is crowned with three small strokes. The previous two (vav and yod) are inclined, reconnecting [4] with the zayin at its base.

According to the Sephardic tradition, the chin is composed of three yods: the one on the right tilts [5] slightly, the middle one is similar to the first, and the distance between the two remains constant [6] from top to base. Due to its tilt, the middle yod connects [7] to the third yod at its base, while the rightmost yod does not directly connect to them. However, they are all united by the base [8] of the letter. The base of the chin is narrower than the total width of the heads, and it tilts to the right.

The top [1] and the right leg [2] form a dalèt. As for the left leg, it takes the shape of an inverted vav, attached to the top.

According to Sephardic writing, this dalèt is often replaced by a rèch.

CHAPTER XXII
A Being on a Journey...

In the entirety of this book, we have addressed Hasidism, Kabbalah, Hebrew meditation, Talmud, and Midrash. The cultural and religious horizon underlying all of these texts and issues is Judaism.

In this journey through letters and words, in these words whose letters we have learned to read, one essential question has accompanied us: What is a "Jew"?

The term "Jew" comes from the Hebrew yéhoudi, which is derived from Yéhouda. The name Yéhouda designates several different things.

Initially, it is the name of the fourth son that Jacob had with Leah (Genesis 29:35), whose name the biblical text derives from the verb lehodot, which means "to give thanks."

Consequently, the place of residence of this tribe became the land of Yéhouda, in French: "Judea," and its inhabitants are the Yéhoudim or, in French: "the Jews."

The similarity between Yéhouda and "Judea," a term attributed by the Romans, is better understood in German, for example: Jude, Juden.

This return to Hebrew, without necessarily proceeding with a geographical and historical analysis, makes us think of the "Jew" from the word-name Yéhouda. But this name, regardless of which, says something beyond Leah's thanksgiving.

The name Yéhouda is written with three letters: yod-hé-vav-dalèt-hé.

In the previous studies, we have prepared ourselves sufficiently to immediately see in this name the Tetragrammaton yod-hé-vav-hé, with the addition of the letter dalèt.

The letter dalèt means "door" in Hebrew, which leads us to conclude that the name Yéhouda means: "to place a door in the Tetragrammaton Name."

The word Yéhoudi, "Jew," is an adjective derived from Yéhouda. Yéhoudim means: "belonging to the tribe of

Yéhouda," or still: "who has the structure of the word Yéhouda," which we can phrase as follows: "The Jew is a person who places a door in the Tetragrammaton Name." Everything we have said in the previous chapters about the Name can serve as a commentary on our proposition. However, we will add here an explanation about the Name, an explanation that must precede and introduce all the other comments.

The Tetragrammaton, four letters without vowels, is written with three letters yod-hé-vav (the hé is repeated twice), which express the present, the past, and the future: hové, haya, yéhé. Also, one can say that the Tetragrammaton is an eternally futurized present, propelled forward by the letter yod (which, in front of a verb, indicates the future): yod, hové.

The door in the Name is, then, a door in time, in a time that does not accept the "now." (It is necessary to remember that Hebrew does not have the verb "to be" in the present.)

Being a Jew—yéhoudi—is opening the door to a present that never remains present, a door that breaks the present to project itself into the past and the future.

Being a Jew is entering into the heart of the possibilities of time, incorporating into such possibilities the three temporal dimensions—past, present, and future, memory, life, and hope.

In this temporization of time, the Jew declares the impossible fixation in the identical and denounces the concept of identity. The Tetragrammaton Name says that "to be" means "to have to be," and the Jew penetrates this deviation, which is the foundation of time itself.

The word "Jew," understood from Yéhouda, means that definitive identity is an illusion and invites us to think "beyond the principle of identity...". The Jew is, then, "Semitic," a descendant of the first son of Noah, Chem, whose name means... "Name."

The descendants of the "Name" receive the revelation of the Tetragrammaton Name, a Name in movement, a Name that escapes the phonetic vibrations and refuses to echo in an "it is said."

Being a Jew immersed in the Name is, in fact, asserting the will to remain outside a definition, outside a concept. This condition is not understood as a refusal to exist; on the contrary, this multiple raising of barriers in language is a choice of existence that is understood as the continuous invention of oneself. There is, here, an ethical stance, grounded in an internal awareness that one can be different. On a collective level, this is translated into a set of practices and rites that are not the lifeless repetition of a past, but the untying of words and things, opposing the petrification of time and space

Made in the USA
Monee, IL
06 April 2025

15273147R00115